ESSAYS ON
PROFESSIONALISM

Frederick K. Slicker

WELCOME FROM THE CHIEF

On behalf of the entire Oklahoma Supreme Court, it is my great honor, privilege and pleasure to welcome you to the practice of law, a noble calling and honorable profession.

Being a lawyer is a special privilege. As a lawyer, you will be an advisor, an evaluator, an advocate and a representative for clients in some of the most difficult and emotional times of their lives. You will also be of an officer of the legal system and a public citizen with special responsibilities for the quality of justice and for the continued improvement in the Rule of Law.

Honesty, integrity and mutual respect for others will be expected of you. You will undoubtedly be challenged by the facts and by the law in seeking to resolve your client's disputes. You may also be faced with difficult moral and ethical dilemmas, which will require you to exercise sensitive professional and moral judgments. In resolving those issues, you should ask yourself: Is my proposed action legal? Is it professional? Is it right? Will I be honored to have taken that action?

These are challenging but exciting times. The legal profession provides a stabilizing force which secures the fundamental rights of life, liberty, property and equal justice for all. As a new member of the legal profession, you will be among those who shape the future of the law and who insure fairness and justice for all. Welcome and best wishes.

For the Court
John E. Reif, Chief Justice
Oklahoma Supreme Court

ABOUT THE COVER

The cover consists of an image of the bronze front doors of the United States Supreme Court. Each of the doors is comprised of four panels depicting major events in the Western Civilization evolution of the Rule of Law. Three of the eight events depicted involve the publication of the *Corpus Juris* by Roman Emperor Justinian in the sixth century, the adoption of the Magna Carta by the King of England in 1215 and the seminal Supreme Court decision in *Marbury v. Madison* in 1803. The importance of an independent judiciary is a key message of these panels. These eight events could not have happened without the scholarship and advocacy of early representatives of the legal profession. The emphasis is the resolution of disputes through negotiation and litigation rather than through force, violence or war. Resolving conflicts without violence requires collegiality, professionalism and mutual respect. The golden color of the doors implies to me that the Golden Rule is inherent in and an essential quality in the preservation of the Rule of Law.

ISBN: 978-1-942451-03-7
eBook: 978-1-942451-09-9
Published by
Yorkshire Publishing
6271 E. 120th Court
Suite 200
Tulsa, OK 74137
www.yorkshirepublishing.com

Text Design: Lisa Simpson
www.SimpsonProductions.net

FORWARD

Essays on Professionalism is a project of the Tulsa County Bar Association. *Essays* is a compilation of articles on topics of professionalism in the legal profession written by Frederick K. Slicker over a period of more than 10 years. Most of these articles have appeared in the <u>Tulsa Lawyer</u>, a publication of the Tulsa County Bar Association. The purpose of *Essays* is to emphasize the importance to individual lawyers and to the legal profession as a whole of the qualities and characteristics fundamental to the profession.

INDEX

Professionalism and Ethics Resources

Oklahoma Bar Association

OBA's **Definition of Professionalism** www.okbar.org/members/ethicscounsel

OBA's **Lawyer's Creed** www.okbar.org/members/ethicscounsel

OBA's **Standards of Professionalism** www.okbar.org/members/ethicscounsel

OBA Ethics Opinions www.okbar.org/members/ethicscounsel

Free ethics advice for OBA Members: OBA Ethics Counsel: 405-416-7055

American Bar Association

ABA Center for Professional Responsibility www.americanbar.org/professionalism

ABA Formal Ethics Opinions

ABA Model Rules of Professional Responsibility

Free ethics research for ABA members: 800-285-2221: Ethic-Search@americanbar.org

Other Resources

Georgia Chief Justice's Commission on Professionalism: 404-225-5042: www.gabar.org/cjcp

PROFESSIONALISM: WHAT IS IT?

In 1997, the American Bar Association published a pamphlet entitled *"Promoting Professionalism,"* which unfortunately is now out of print. In that pamphlet, the ABA remarked:

> "Professionalism embraces a larger field than ethics. Ethics is a set of rules that lawyers *must* obey with sanctions for disobedience. Professionalism encompasses not only what a lawyer *must* or *must not* do, but also what a lawyer *should* do to serve a client and the public and how it should be done."

Nevertheless, defining "professionalism" has been elusive. Even the ABA's pamphlet was not able to come to a consensus on a definition of "professionalism." In fact, despite a significant search, I found no universally accepted definition of professionalism. Let me suggest the following definition:

Professionalism is living a life of personal integrity, professional competence and mutual respect for others. Professionalism involves:

(1) Doing what is morally right; and

(2) Representing clients with honesty, integrity and competence; and

(3) Treating clients, opposing counsel, the courts, and others with civility and common courtesy; and

(4) Complying with the law and the Rules of Professional Conduct; and

(5) Serving the client and the public interest by promoting respect for the Rule of Law.

This definition embodies five basic principles of professionalism which are generally recognized to be include in the criteria for accepted professional behavior: Integrity, competence, civility, compliance and service to others.

Integrity

Personal honesty and integrity of lawyers is the cornerstone of the legal system, without which no system of law can prevail. When lawyers are not honest, particularly in papers filed in court, the rule of law is jeopardized. If the courts cannot rely upon the honesty of the lawyers that practice before them, the system of law itself is placed at risk. In its pamphlet, *Promoting Professionalism*, the ABA stated:

> "No element of professionalism is more important than ethics... The ethical integrity of the lawyer must be our profession's hallmark and call for public confidence. Ethics is not just a set of rules. It is a value system, a mind-set, a responsibility that must remain constant in the lawyer's consciousness."

On November 17, 1989, the OBA Board of Governors adopted the **Lawyer's Creed** which reads in part:

> "In my dealings with the Court and with counsel, as well as with others, my word is my bond. . . ."

The **Lawyer's Creed** was revised by the OBA on March 8, 2008 to include reference to the OBA's **Standards of Professionalism**. The full text of the OBA's **Lawyer's Creed** can be found at www. okbar.org/members/ethicscounsel.

On November 20, 2002, the OBA Board of Governors adopted the **Standards of Professionalism,** which were also adopted by the Oklahoma Judicial Conference on December 20, 2002. Section 1.2 of these **Standards** states as follows:

> "1.2   A lawyer's word should be his or her bond. We will not knowingly misstate, distort or improperly exaggerate any fact, opinion or legal authority, and will not improperly permit our silence or inaction to mislead anyone. . ."

The full text of the **Standards** is at www.okbar.org/members/ethicscounsel.

Despite these platitudes, too often some lawyers do exactly the opposite. Some lawyers do misstate, do exaggerate, do distort and do mislead, all in an effort to win the argument, to carry the day. When will we learn that personal integrity and honesty are the foundation upon which our profession and our system of law depend?

Professional Competence

Rule 1.1 of the Oklahoma Rules of Professional Conduct states: "A lawyer shall provide competent representation to a client. Competent representation requires the legal knowledge, skill, thoroughness, and preparation reasonably necessary for the representation." It is not an accident that competence is the first of the Rules. Clients expect their lawyer to know the law and how to apply it. But competence means more than just having a basic knowledge of the law, because all people are presumed to know the law. Competence implies proficiency in applying the rules of law to the facts in question in an effort to solve the problems facing the client. Competence, therefore, embodies more than just education and knowledge. Competence consists of the ability to apply the knowledge of the law and pro-cedures with experience, preparation, diligence, determination and commitment.

Competence, however, does not mean perfection in any matter, but competence does mean that lawyers are expected to seek with diligence and determination the content, meaning and purpose of the law, so that their knowledge of the law and facts is applied with experience and wisdom in helping solve the client's problems.

Mutual Respect

The Golden Rule, that is, "Do unto others as you would have them do unto you," has been a universally accepted standard of conduct in most cultures throughout all generations of man as a guiding principal for proper civil conduct. In the legal profession, we often use the term "civility" as a short hand way to refer to this accepted standard of professional conduct.

The ABA's *Promoting Professionalism* quotes Justice Anthony M. Kennedy in his address to the 1997 Annual ABA Meeting as follows:

"Civility is the mark of an accomplished and superb profes-sional, but it is more even than this. It is an end in itself. Civility has deep roots in the idea of respect for the individual. . . respect for the dignity and worth of a fellow human being."

Mutual respect for the client, for opposing counsel, for the courts and for the rule of law is the end that professionalism embraces.

The **Lawyer's Creed** referred to above includes the following:

"I revere the Law, the System [of Justice] and the Profession, and I pledge that in my private practice and professional life, and in my dealings with members of the Bar, I will uphold the dignity and respect of each in my behavior towards others. . .

"In all dealings with members of the Bar, I will be guided by a fundamental sense of integrity and fair play. . .

"I recognize that a desire to prevail must be tempered with civility. Rude behavior hinders effective advocacy. . ."

The **Standards of Professionalism** referred to above includes the following standard:

"<u>3.1a</u> We will be civil, courteous, respectful, honest and fair in communicating with adversaries, orally and in writing."

Despite these platitudes, all too often, lawyers practice Rambo tactics which foster antagonism, rancor, excessive aggressiveness and a win-at-all-costs approach gone wild. Many of those that engage in this extreme form of conduct sometimes even believe that our clients want a gladiator, take-no-prisoners attitude against their opponents and their opponent's counsel. The exact opposite is actually true. Clients do not want a fight or a case. Clients want their problems solved quickly and efficiently. While they do want to win, they do not want endless and expensive arguments. Problem-solving is not enhanced by mean-spirited personal attacks on others or rude and inconsiderate behavior.

<u>Compliance</u>

Compliance means that lawyers will follow the law in furthering the interests of their clients. But compliance also means that lawyers will also comply with the Rules of Professional Conduct and the generally accepted **Standards of Professionalism.**

Service

The legal profession requires that each lawyer embrace service to others as an essential part of the practice of law. Service means contributing time, energy, knowledge and experience to community, civic, religious, not-for-profit and similar organizations. Service also means providing representation to those that need but do not have the means to pay for legal representation. Giving to those that are less fortunate is a fundamental value of the legal profession.

Conclusion

Professionalism is a life style, not a set of rules or principles. Professionalism embodies a commitment to personal and professional integrity and honesty in all dealings with others. Professionalism expects lawyers to be competent in their knowledge of the law, but also in their attitude and approach to the application of those rules in an effort to solve the client's problems within the framework of the legal system. Professionalism embodies a spirit of service to the client but also embraces service to others who are less fortunate and to the system of law itself. All too often, there is a gap between what lawyers say and what lawyers do. It is the duty and obligation of every lawyer to embrace and enhance the core values of professionalism, to increase the respect by the public for the law and the profession and to advance the rule of law. The public deserves nothing less.

A TALE OF TWO LAWYERS:

A SUMMARY

A Tale of Two Lawyers, 91 Nw. U. L. Rev. 615, Carrington, Paul (1997) compares and contrasts the moral and professional qualities of Abraham Lincoln and Charles Sumner in an effort to demonstrate what constitutes a successful and professional lawyer. Professor Carrington observes:

> "The comparison of Lincoln and Sumner demonstrates that success in gaining the maturity and professional judgment associated with a sound knowledge of self will not depend on one's law school grade point average or other accoutrements of academic status. Indeed, **in professional work in law, integrity and mature judgment often prevail over genius.**"

Professor Carrington compares Lincoln with Sumner, focusing on the moral and professional characteristics of each in an effort to reveal what constitutes a successful lawyer.

LINCOLN	SUMNER
Born into poverty in Illinois	Born into privilege in Boston
Little formal education	Educated at Harvard and Harvard Law School
Read a few great books	Taught at Harvard Law School; studied in France
Had no legal mentors	Was mentored by the most elite lawyers
Represented all kinds of cases	Represented only the Boston elite in high profile commercial cases
Argued hundreds of contested appeals	No record of appellate work
Knew himself; knew his deficiencies	Did not know himself; did not acknowledge any deficiencies

Was extraordinarily mature early	Showed "morbid juvenility"
Cared for his clients	Did not care for people
Demonstrated awesome integrity	Was self-centered; morally superior
Enjoyed humor	Showed little humor
Was humble	Was arrogant
Often quoted the Bible	Referred to obscure ancient texts
Was a problem-solver	Was a problem-perpetuator
Was self-controlled	Left friction in his wake
Exercised wise judgment	Had no common sense
Was self-restrained	Bullied and dehumanized opponents
Compromised immaterial points	Would not compromise ever
Worked very hard	Left hard work to the clerks
Assigned credit to others	Took all the credit; assigned blamed to others
Was practical	Was theoretical and moralizing
Was respectful to all	Was haughty, arrogant, domineering
Was self-disciplined	Lacked self-discipline
Had great common sense	Was morally arrogant
Focused on substance	Focused on the petty
Was a public servant	Was unfit for public service
Sought to uncover motives	Was not interested in motives
Was thoughtful, caring, compassionate	Was embittered and critical
Was peaceful	Was hostile and antagonistic
Was an excellent mediator and negotiator	Was morally superior and intellectually arrogant; would not compromise
Was a superb, effective lawyer	Was ineffective and not a good lawyer

Professor Carrington acknowledges that moral education in law school has "produced limited results." **Wisdom and virtue do not come from formal education.** Wisdom comes from experience and thoughtful reflection. Virtue is inherent in all people; but pride, arrogance and evil can overcome good intentions, unless each individual rests his or her life on a high moral code. Being a person of "good moral character" is a prerequisite for becoming and being an Oklahoma lawyer. See 5 OK Stat. Section 3. It is a prerequisite to being a professional lawyer too.

Professor Carrington argues that self-knowledge, civic virtue and moral integrity are the foundations of successful lawyering. Each individual lawyer must value those high moral principles. Each individual is responsible for his or her conduct. "They must train themselves or not for public duties. Teachers can help, but **no law school can make virtuous, self-restrained, tolerant, prudent men and women of students who do not value those traits.**"

Professor Carrington finally argues that:

"It is therefore the public duty of lawyers to know themselves, to know and discount their passions, their pride, and their prejudices. More than anything one can learn by formal study of law, useful lawyering requires professional judgment animated and informed by appreciation of the values and moral aspirations of the people whom public lawyers assist in governing themselves."

In summary, Lincoln was compassionate, caring and interested in his clients. Lincoln's dictum in private practice and in politics was: "Never plead what you need not, lest you oblige yourself to prove what you cannot." What Lincoln did so effectively was to give away "what he couldn't get and keep. By giving away six points and arguing the seventh, he traded everything which would give him the least aid" for the one thing that secured victory.

Sumner, on the other hand, "has never sown, planted, gathered, fed, but has always destroyed, embittered, ruined and cursed." Even Sumner's own friend and advisor acknowledges that Sumner "was unfit for public service."

The professional lawyer will display a commitment to a high moral core, not by speaking but by acting upon the core values of mutual respect, virtue, self-restraint, tolerance and wisdom. As lawyers, it is not only our privilege to help others resolve their legal difficulties, but it is our duty to demonstrate sound professional judgment, respect for others and civic responsibility. Nothing less is acceptable.

CHARACTERISTICS OF THE PROFESSIONAL LAWYER

There is much debate and no consensus about what constitutes "professionalism" or even what characteristics are to be found in the "professional" lawyer.

In 2006, the Oklahoma Bar Association adopted the following definition:

"Professionalism for lawyers and judges requires honestly, integrity, competence, civility and public service."

All would agree that these characteristic are required for a lawyer to be viewed as a "professional," but most would argue that more is required.

On April 16, 2015, the Tulsa County Bar Association unanimously adopted the following new definition:

"Professionalism for judges and lawyers means possessing, demonstrating and promoting the highest standards of Character, Competence, Compliance, Courage, Civility and Citizenship."

On June 25, 2015, the Oklahoma Bar Association Professionalism Committee adopted this same definition of professionalism and recommended approval by the OBA Board of Governors.

Professionalism requires that lawyers not only actively demonstrate the characteristics of professionalism in their own lives and practices, but also that they encourage and promote those concepts of professionalism in others. Professionalism is not a passive concept, and professionalism is not simply hollow, high-minded phrases which never see the light of day in the daily practice of law. Rather, professionalism requires active and intentional effort.

The professional lawyer is a person of high moral <u>character</u> and personal integrity. The professional lawyer is honest, trustworthy, dependable and responsible. The professional lawyer daily demonstrates a commitment to high moral principles, including mutual respect and fairness to all.

The professional lawyer is <u>competent</u>. The competent lawyer knows the facts and the law and uses good judgment and experience to further the client's interests. Competence requires that the lawyer listen carefully to the client, respond accurately to the client's questions and pursue the client's goals and objectives with diligence, reason and good faith.

The professional lawyer <u>complies</u> with both procedural and substantive laws, rules and regulations; observes the Rules of Professional Conduct and follows the Standards of Professionalism. The professional lawyer does not seek an unfair advantage by playing games in discovery or by filing motions out of time or under circumstances where the opponent does not have a fair opportunity to respond. The professional lawyer does not change documents without telling the lawyer on the other side of the transaction the changes made. The professional lawyer plays by the rules and plays fairly.

The professional lawyer demonstrates <u>courage</u> by doing what is right, even when doing so is highly unpopular or runs counter to long-held community standards. Sometimes the professional lawyer is required to challenge laws in order to secure justice for the lawyer's client. Often the professional lawyer takes positions that expose the lawyer and the lawyer's family to great personal risk. One example of courage involves prosecutors enforcing the laws against organized crime bosses. Other examples of courage include the defense lawyer representing a highly unpopular defendant or the civil rights lawyer seeking to change unfair or unconstitutional community beliefs.

The professional lawyer is <u>civil</u>. The professional lawyer demonstrates respect, courtesy and collegiality to the clients, the opponents, the courts and their staffs. Civility often dampens emotions and reduces the friction between the parties, so that reason and mutually agreed solutions can be achieved. Civility is not a sign of weakness. Quite the contrary. Civility reflects confidence and fairness. Acting with civility facilitates problem-solving and dispute resolution.

The professional lawyer is a <u>good citizen</u> who volunteers time and effort to improve the community and to insure equal justice for all. Good citizenship means that the professional lawyer takes a leadership role in not-for-profit, community and faith-based organizations. Whether a public servant or a private citizen, the professional lawyer is a citizen with a special role in preserving and improving the Rule of Law.

On the other hand, the lawyers who act unprofessionally typically adopt a win-at-all-costs, Rambo attitude. They often engage in extreme behavior, justifying their arrogance, attitude and misconduct by asserting a misguided and distorted view of the lawyer's duty of zealous representation of the clients. They usually demonstrate some of the following characteristics:

They are rude, offensive or abrasive.

They are discourteous, disrespectful or dishonest.

They engage in harassing, humiliating or embarrassing conduct.

They are sleazy, obnoxious or vulgar.

They are unprincipled, immoral or uncivilized.

They are overly combative, aggressive or competitive

They use disparaging remarks and name calling.

They disregard procedural rules and respond out of time.

They omit or hide documents required in discovery.

They misrepresent the facts, mischaracterize the record or mis-quote the law.

They use false, reckless or misleading statements.

They omit important facts, spin the truth or exaggerate the facts.

They are antagonistic, annoying and obstructive.

They are acrimonious and overly zealous.

They are arrogant, egotistic or self-absorbed.

They are uncompromising and deliberatively uncooperative.

They create friction, animosity and distrust.

They represent half-truths as the whole truth.

Lawyers who resort to unprofessional tactics usually hurt their clients, cause unnecessary expenses and destroy any chance of their having a good name or reputation. "A good name is more desirable than great riches; to be esteemed is better than silver or gold." Proverbs 22:1 (NIV). There is simply no place in our profession for those that abuse or game the system or resort to the attitudes and characteristics of the unprofessional lawyer described above.

The legal profession needs men and women who demonstrate and promote high moral character, competence, compliance, courage, civility and citizenship. These lawyers are the fabric which upholds American dream and the Rule of Law. Our clients and our profession depend upon the professional lawyer. They deserve nothing less. We owe them nothing less.

A NEW DEFINITION OF PROFESSIONALISM

There is general agreement among the leaders of the legal profession that enhancing professionalism is among the most important functions of the organized bar. Yet, there has been a general decline in the public's attitude towards lawyers and the legal profession. *Rethinking Professionalism,* Terrill and Wildman, 41 Emory L. J. 403. A 2008 Gallup Poll found that only 18% of those surveyed would rate the honesty and ethical standards of lawyers as high or very high. This poll is not new news. The proliferation of lawyer jokes that attack the ethics and truthfulness of lawyers and the portrayal of lawyers on TV and in movies as tricksters or worse continue to paint a bleak picture of the legal profession, at least as viewed by the public.

In 1984, the American Bar Association Board of Governors established the Commission on Professionalism. In 1998, Jerome J. Shestack, then President of the ABA, committed the ABA on a course to enhance public attitudes toward lawyers and the legal profession. *Taking Professionalism Seriously,* 84 ABA Journal 70 (1998). ABA President Shestack's description of professionalism consisted of six criteria: (1) ethics and integrity, (2) competence combined with independence, (3) continuing legal education, (4) civility, (5) obligations to the justice system, and (6) pro bono service. 84 ABA Journal 70-71 (1998)

In the late 1990s a national professionalism movement emerged, led by the Chief Justice of the Georgia Supreme Court, who established a Commission on Professionalism in coordination with the ABA's Center for Professional Responsibility. Virtually all state bar associations adopted lawyer creeds and standards of professionalism as part of that program. Despite this enormous effort, the public's perception of the legal profession continues to decline. Incredibly, the organized bar still has not even been able to adopt a universally accepted definition of professionalism.

In late December, 2013, the ABA's Standing Committee on Professionalism published *Essential Qualities of the Professional Lawyer*, Paul Haskins, Editor (*"Professional Lawyer"*). *Professional Lawyer* recognized that "there is no single universally accepted definition of professionalism; and there is even no consensus on the constituent pieces of professionalism, an amorphous concept." (*Professional Lawyer*, p. xxvi)

For Harvard Dean Roscoe Pound, "professionalism" refers to "a group *pursuing a learned art as a common calling in the spirit of public service*---no less a public service because it may incidentally be a means of livelihood. *Pursuit of the learned art in the spirit of public service is the primary purpose."* (Emphasis added.)

For one member of the Florida bar, professionalism means "to represent clients and serve the community in a dignified, courteous and competent manner, to demonstrate character as an honest, reasonable and respectful advocate and to be committed to upholding the honor and integrity of the law and our system of justice." See *Defining Professionalism: I Know It When I See It?* Keith W. Rizzardi, 79 Florida B. J. No. 7, July/August, 2005, Note 10.

The ABA Standing Committee on Professionalism recently issued a White Paper calling on the organized bar to re-examine the meaning of professionalism. In that White Paper, the Committee suggested the following elements of professionalism by way of the acronym SERVE as follows:

S Support of the legal system; and

E Exemplify professionalism through teaching, technology and training; and

R Reaffirm access to the legal system, promoting justice through a dispute resolution system that is available to all; and

V Value our place in society, integrating our core values of professionalism in each representation to provide our clients with real value while ensuring that we and our associates maintain professional values and act with integrity; and

E Embrace professional excellence while establishing an equilibrium in lawyers' lives.

The acronym, **SERVE,** sounds nice, but in my view this description of professionalism falls woefully short of defining what the "core values" of professionalism are and provides little help and no guidance to the practicing lawyer in the trenches when faced with professional challenges.

A much better approach was adopted on April 20, 2006, by the Oklahoma Bar Association's Board of Governors, at the urging of the OBA's Professionalism Committee, which adopted the following definition: **"Professionalism for lawyers and judges requires honestly, integrity, competence, civility and public service."** This definition has served OK lawyers well since its adoption, but even this definition: (1) omits several basic core values of character while highlighting honesty and integrity; (2) leaves out each lawyer's duty of independent professional judgment; (3) omits any reference to a life time commitment to excellence; (4) excludes any reference to continuing legal education; and most importantly (5) makes no mention of compliance with the Rules of Professional Conduct. Further, the OBA's definition conspicuously makes no reference to the OBA's **Lawyer's Creed**, which it adopted on November 17, 1887 and amended on March 8, 2008, or to the OBA's **Standards of Professionalism** which it adopted on November 20, 2002, or to any other similar creed or code of conduct.

There is a big difference between ethics and professionalism. Ethics, as reflected in the Oklahoma Rules of Professional Conduct, tells lawyers what they <u>must</u> do. Professionalism, as contemplated by the **Lawyer's Creed** and the **Standards of Professionalism** and other similar codes of conduct, tell lawyers what they <u>should</u> do. Even so, professionalism must at least include the minimum mandatory standards of conduct described in the Rules of Professional Conduct and incorporate the aspirational spirit of the **Lawyer's Creed** and the **Standards of Professionalism**.

I propose adopting a new more inclusive definition of Professionalism as follows: **"Professionalism for judges and lawyers means possessing, demonstrating and promoting the highest standards of Character, Competence, Compliance, Civility and Citizenship."**

Demonstrating these five qualities means that lawyers need to embrace them and live them out, both professionally and in their personal lives. Promoting these qualities means not only that lawyers must act according to these five concepts, but also that each lawyer should affirmatively and actively encourage other lawyers to do so too. Meeting the highest levels of these five concepts means that lawyers will strive to improve and to achieve the best of what is embodied by these five concepts. Finally, these five concepts define the essence of professionalism in an easily remembered expression: the five C's.

Character means that lawyers are committed to generally accepted high moral principles and fundamental core values that govern their private, professional and public lives. Some of these core values include:

1. To be honest

2. To act with integrity

3. To be moral

4. To be trustworthy

5. To be reasonable

6. To be responsible

7. To be honorable

8. To be punctual

9. To be dependable

10. To be virtuous

11. To care about their clients

12. To be faithful and loyal to their clients

13. To enhance the Rule of Law

14. To be a good example

15. To live a life of high moral values

<u>Competence</u> means that lawyers have the professional skills, knowledge, background and experience to represent their clients in the matters in which the lawyer is engaged. That means that the lawyer will act:

1. To learn the important facts

2. To know the applicable law

3. To understand the dispute

4. To understand the parties

5. To define the positions of the parties

6. To seek efficient solutions

7. To communicate persuasively

8. To advise the client honestly

9. To represent the client faithfully

10. To give the client independent professional advice

11. To trust but verify the client's facts

12. To not contest insignificant matters

13. To negotiate fairly and honestly

14. To be punctual

15. To be prepared

16. To commit to excellence

17. To engage in lifelong learning

Compliance means that the lawyer will act:

1. In compliance with the law

2. In compliance with the Rules of Professional Conduct

3. In compliance with the **Lawyer's Creed**

4. In compliance with the **Standards of Professionalism**

5. To challenge unjust, unfair and unequal laws

6. To seek to improve the law

Civility means that the lawyer will:

1. Respect others

2. Follow the Golden Rule

3. Be courteous

4. Be cooperative

5. Not be rude or offensive

6. Not be abrasive or abusive

7. Not be mean, vulgar or disruptive

8. Not embarrass, humiliate or demean others

Citizenship means that the lawyer will be a good citizen by participating in the political process and:

1. Serve others, especially those in need

2. Render pro bono services to the poor

3. Serve civic and charitable organizations

4. Support churches and faith-based organizations

5. Respect the legal system

6. Support the independence of the judiciary

7. Seek equal justice for all

8. Work to improve the legal system

9. Advance the Rule of Law

Being a lawyer is a privilege, not a right. The practice of law requires that those who represent clients adopt and demonstrate the highest standards of morality and excellence. **"Professionalism for judges and lawyers means possessing, demonstrating and promoting the highest standards of Character, Competence, Compliance, Civility and Citizenship."** These qualities are generally accepted standards of professional conduct and are expected of all lawyers by the clients and the public. We owe our clients, the public and the profession nothing less.

GOOD MORAL CHARACTER: AN ESSENTIAL ELEMENT OF PROFESSIONALISM

I recently proposed a new definition of professionalism: *"Professionalism for lawyers and judges means possessing, demonstrating and promoting Character, Competence, Compliance, Civility and Citizenship."* See <u>Tulsa Lawyer</u>, December 2014. The OBA's current definition is: "Professionalism for lawyers and judges requires **honestly, integrity**, competence, civility and public service." The proposed definition substitutes "character" for "honesty, integrity;" adds the requirement of "compliance" and substitutes "citizenship" for the term "service."

To be sure, honesty and integrity form the bedrock upon which professionalism rests. Nothing in the proposed definition is intended to diminish the importance of honesty and integrity as characteristics required for professionalism. Instead, the purpose of this article is to unwrap what "character" means in the proposed definition of "professionalism."

In Oklahoma, every applicant for admission to the bar has the statutory burden of proving that the applicant qualifies as a person of "good moral character."

"When a person applies to the Supreme Court for admission to the bar, he shall be examined by the Court . . . touching his *fitness and qualifications;* and if, on such examination the Court is satisfied that he is of *good moral character,* and has a competent knowledge of the law, and sufficient general learning, an oath of office shall be administered to him. . ." 5 OK Stat. Section 14 (Emphasis added.)

Oklahoma statutes do not define the term "good moral character," but the statutory oath of office required to be taken by each applicant for admission to the Bar gives us some hints. Each applicant must swear to:

> "support, protect, and defend the constitution of the United States of America, and the constitution of the State of Oklahoma; that you will *do no falsehood* or consent that any be done in court . . . you will *not wittingly, willingly or knowingly promote,* sue or procure to be sued, *any false or unlawful suit . . .* but will act in the office of attorney in this court according to your *best learning and discretion,* with all good fidelity as well to the court as to your client, so help you God." 5 OK Stat. Section 2 (Emphasis added.)

Thus, each lawyer must promise under oath to:

1. "Do no falsehood;"

2. "Not wittingly, willingly or knowingly promote" false suits;

3. Exercise his or her "best learning"; and

4. Act with "discretion."

Oklahoma statutes which define the duties of being an attorney and counselor at law also provide hints as to what constitutes "good moral character" by the following list:

> "First. To maintain . . . the **respect** due to the said courts...and at all times obey all lawful orders . . .

"Third. To employ . . . such means only as are **consistent with truth,** and **never to seek to mislead** the judges by any artifice or false statements of facts or law . . .

"Fifth. To **abstain from all offensive personalities,** and to advance no fact prejudicial to the honor or reputation of a party or witness unless required by justice . . ." 5 OK Stat. Section 3 (Emphasis added.)

<u>Rule 1.3</u> of the Rules Governing Disciplinary Proceedings, 5 OK Stat. Ch.1-App 1-A, Rule 1.3 provides that the:

"commission by any lawyer of *any act contrary to prescribed standards of conduct,* whether in the course of his professional capacity, or otherwise, which act would *reasonably be found to bring discredit upon the legal profession,* shall be grounds for disciplinary action, whether or not the act is a felony or misdemeanor, or a crime at all..." (Emphasis added.)

I believe that any definition of professionalism must, as a minimum, include the statutory <u>qualifications</u> of a lawyer, the statutory <u>duties</u> of a lawyer and the statutory <u>oath</u> required to be taken by every lawyer in order to get an Oklahoma law license and should not permit conduct which is subject to professional discipline.

Consequently, in place of "honesty, integrity" I have substituted the term "character" in the proposed new definition of professionalism. Why? Because good moral character is a requirement in order to obtain and retain an Oklahoma law license and because I believe that good moral character involves more than honesty and integrity, even though without honesty and integrity, there can be no professionalism at all.

So what constitutes "good moral character?" Honesty and integrity are absolutely essential characteristics to be included in the term "good moral character," but other positive characteristics which I expect from a person of good moral character are not included in the terms honesty and integrity, such as:

1. A person of good moral character should be <u>responsible</u>, which means the lawyer is dependable and does what he or she says when he or she says it. A promise given is a promised kept. The person obeys the law and his or her other duties and obligations to others. His or her word is a bond.

2. A person of good moral character is <u>trustworthy</u>, which means that the person can be trusted with the problems and property of others. The person is a promise keeper and fulfills the duties of a fiduciary.

3. A person of good moral character is <u>virtuous</u>, which means that the person does what is right and seeks justice for all in furtherance of a high moral code.

4. A person of good moral character is <u>fair</u>, which means that the person treats others without prejudice and seeks equality for all.

5. A person of good moral character is <u>loyal</u>, which means that the person puts the interests of others before his or her own self-interest.

6. A person of good moral character is <u>respected</u>, which means that the person treats others with honor and

dignity and has a good reputation for fairness among his or her peers.

7. A person of good moral character is <u>honorable</u>, which means that the person brings honor to himself or herself by making decisions and by acting in accordance with a high moral code.

8. A person of good moral character is a <u>servant,</u> which means that the person works for the benefit of others. He or she is known for the good works that are done for others. He or she walks the walk.

Justice Frankfurter noted that lawyers should possess the qualities of "truth speaking, of a high sense of honor, of granite discretion, of the strictest observance of fiduciary responsibility . . . *Schware v. Board of Bar Examiners*, 353 US 232, 247 (Frankfurter, J., concurring.)

Other positive characteristics often included in the definition of "good moral character" are diligence, candor, discretion, respect for others, financial responsibility, knowledge, experience, mental and emotional stability and commitment to the legal system and the judicial process. See *The Good Character Requirement: A Proposal for a Uniform National Standard*, Ratliff, Mark, 36 Tulsa L. Rev. 487, 495 (2000) ("Ratliff").

There are problems with using "good moral character" as a qualification for admission to the bar, including:

1. There is no clear commonly accepted list of requirements for a finding of good moral character; and

2. The proof required to establish good moral character is fuzzy; and

3. The criteria used are almost impossible to measure; and

4. Evidence of good moral character is difficult to quantify; and

5. The possibility of abuse and inconsistency is significant.

Historically, state bar associations have excluded otherwise qualified "problem" applicants for admission to the bar, because they were deemed to be "radicals, religious fanatics, divorcees, fornicators and individuals who challenged the profession's anticompetitive ethical canons," so that discrimination on the basis of gender, ethnicity, religion, political belief and economic status occurred on occasion. *The Troubling Rise of the Legal Profession's Good Moral Character*, Swisher, Keith, 82 St. John L. Rev. 1037, 1042 ("Swisher"). Consequently, Professor Swisher argues that the current process of character assessment is fundamentally flawed, inconsistent, overwhelmingly baseless, arbitrary, discriminatory, intellectually dishonest, oppressive and unbecoming of the learned legal profession.

Proving that an applicant possesses good moral character has instead become a demonstration of the absence of prior bad acts, such as unlawful conduct, academic misconduct, making false or incomplete statements in the bar application process, employment misconduct, dishonesty, substance abuse, bankruptcy or mental illness. See Ratliff at 496. See also Swisher at 1043-44.

There is a big difference between applying for a law license where the applicant must bear the affirmative burden of proving his or her "good moral character," on the one hand, and overcoming the presumption that the lawyer facing disbarment has already demonstrated "good moral character," on the other. Nevertheless, "good moral character" is a continuing qualification requirement for holding and keeping an Oklahoma law license. *OBA v Booth*, 441 P.2d 405 (OK 1966) ("good moral character is a continuing qualification . . . necessary to entitle one to continue as a member of the Bar."). Booth was disbarred for unspecified conduct which, due to a legal technicality, was not criminal but did involve moral turpitude, was "unprofessional in the extreme" and demonstrated that he was "unfit and untrustworthy" to practice law. Several other Oklahoma Supreme Court cases affirm that various types of bad conduct do not meet the "good moral character" standard. For example, wrongful use of the client's money, *OBA v Kessler*, 573 P.2d 1214 (OK 1978); commingling client's funds with the lawyer's private funds, *OBA v. Raskin*, 642 P.2d 261 (OK 1982); felony conviction for conspiracy to establish gambling and prostitution business involving moral turpitude, *OBA v. Grayson*, 560 P.2d 566 (OK 1977); solicitation of a bribe by a judge, *OBA v. James*, 463 P.2d 972 (OK 1969); solicitation of sex in exchange for legal services, *OBA v. Gassaway*, 196 P.3d 495 (OK 2008); and sexual misconduct constituting the misdemeanor of outraging public decency, *OBA v. Murdock*, 236 P.3d 107 (OK 2010).

The conclusion is inescapable. Professionalism absolutely requires honesty and integrity, but professionalism requires much more than honesty and integrity as an embodiment of "good moral character." Professionalism also requires that lawyers be responsible, trustworthy, dependable, loyal, fair and honorable and that lawyers not bring discredit upon themselves or the legal profession by engaging in conduct that does not meet the "good moral character" test. Only when each lawyer meets the requirements of having and demonstrating good moral character will the legal profession secure its rightful place in the advancement of equality, justice and the Rule of Law.

HONESTY:
THE FIRST DUTY OF EVERY LAWYER

The February, 2008 issue of the ABA Journal contained an ethics article that really disturbed me. The cover contained a caption, "When is it OK to lie?" and the article was entitled, "When the Truth Can Wait." (ABA Journal, Feb. 2008 at Page 26). The article described an ethics complaint filed against a very prominent Portland, Oregon plaintiffs' attorney engaged in representing several chiropractors in a racketeering and fraud case involving alleged fraudulent workers' compensation claims. The lawyer sought to find out how medical reviews were conducted, believing that he would discover evidence of dishonest and criminal activity. In the pursuit of exposing wrongful conduct, he called various medical review companies and represented to them that he was either a medical doctor or a chiropractor. Based upon what he learned in these calls, he filed suit against these companies. A lawyer for one of the companies filed an ethics complaint.

The Oregon State Bar ruled that the plaintiffs' lawyer had violated several provisions of the Oregon Code of Professional Responsibility prohibiting lawyers from engaging in dishonesty, fraud, deceit or misrepresentation while engaged in representing a client, even when the activities were conducted in an effort to uncover dishonest and criminal activity. The Oregon Supreme Court agreed in *In re Gatti*, 8 P.3rd 966 (OR 2000), and issued a public reprimand. Subsequently, the Oregon Supreme Court amended the ethics rules in Oregon to permit lawyers to advise and supervise others who engage in deceit or misrepresentation while conducting investigations if the lawyer acts in good faith believing that there is a reasonable possibility that unlawful conduct has, is or will take place in the future. It is unclear whether Oregon lawyers can directly engage in deceit or misrepresentation for a noble cause.

Oklahoma has no such exception. The first duty of every lawyer is to tell the truth.

Rule 3.3 deals with candor to tribunals and provides in part that a lawyer shall not:

"(1) knowingly make a false statement of fact or law to a tribunal or fail to correct a false statement of material fact or law previously made to the tribunal by the lawyer;" . . . [or]

"(3) offer evidence the lawyer knows to be false..."

Rule 4.1 deals with truthfulness to third persons other than the lawyer's clients and provides in part that:

"In the course of representing a client a lawyer shall not knowingly:

"(a) make a false statement of material fact or law to a third person; or

"(b) fail to disclose a material fact to a third person when disclosure is necessary to avoid assisting a criminal or fraudulent act by a client unless disclosure is prohibited by Rule 1.6."

Note that a lawyer has a duty to be honest and truthful in dealing with third persons, but the Rule is specifically qualified by the lawyer's duty to retain client confidentiality. Note also that there is no reliance requirement by the third persons, so a violation occurs when the statement is made, even if no one relies or acts on it. To violate the Rule, the statement must be a materially false statement of fact or law. The comment to this Rule makes clear that estimates of price or value and other similar statements made in negotiations that are not generally understood to be "statements of fact" are excluded from the prohibition under the Rule. Comment 1 to the Rule makes clear that repeating a statement attributed to another when the lawyer knows the statement to be false is also prohibited.

Rule 7.1 deals with communications about the lawyer and the lawyer's services and provides that:

"A lawyer shall not make a false or misleading communication about the lawyer or the lawyer's services. A communication is false or misleading if it contains a material misrepresentation of fact or law, or omits a fact necessary to make the communication considered as a whole not materially misleading."

This Rule sounds very much like the anti-fraud provisions of federal securities law under the Securities and Exchange Act of 1934, Rule 10(b)(5), but this Rule is much, much broader than even Rule 10(b)(5). Rule 7.1 has no requirement for a client or a member of the public or even another lawyer to rely on the statement or to be damaged by reason of the falsehood. Again, Rule 7.1 is violated when the false statement is made, even if no one acts upon the statement and even if no one suffers damages by it. Comment 2 to the Rule provides that even "Truthful statements that are misleading are also prohibited by this Rule." Read literally, a misleading statement about the lawyer or the lawyer's services violates the Rule, even if the statement is not material for any purpose.

Rule 8.4 deals with "general unprofessional conduct" and provides in part:

"It is professional misconduct for a lawyer to:

"(b) commit a criminal act that reflects adversely on the lawyer's honesty, trustworthiness or fitness as a lawyer in other respects;

"(c) engage in conduct involving dishonesty, fraud, deceit or misrepresentation; . . ."

In summary, the Oklahoma Rules of Professional Conduct prohibit materially false or misleading statements or omissions made by a lawyer to tribunals and to third persons and when the lawyer is speaking about the lawyer or the lawyer's services. There is no specific prohibition against material or immaterial false or misleading statements or omissions by the lawyer if made to the lawyer's client or to opposing counsel, except where Rule 8.4(c) comes into effect. Even if Rule 8.4(c) applies, there is no requirement that anyone actually rely upon the statement to his or her detriment; and there is no requirement that anyone actually suffer damages as a result of the lawyer's false or misleading statement.

The **Standards of Professionalism** adopted by the OBA's Board of Governors in November, 2002 reinforce the concept that honesty is the lawyer's first duty when dealing with others.

1.2   provides in part that "A lawyer's word should be his or her bond. We will not knowingly misstate, distort or improperly exaggerate any fact, opinion or legal authority."

1.6   provides in part that "Our conduct with clients, opposing counsel, parties, witnesses and the public will be honest, professional and civil."

1.7　provides in part that "Our public communications will reflect appropriate civility, professional integrity, personal dignity and respect ..."

1.8　provides in part that "We will not make statements which are false, misleading, or which exaggerate ..."

2.12　provides that "We will not falsely hold out the possibility of settlement as a means to adjourn discovery or delay trial."

3.1　provides that "We will be civil, courteous, respectful, honest and fair in communicating with adversaries ..."

4.5　provides that "We will never knowingly misrepresent, mischaracterize, misquote, miscite facts or authorities or otherwise engage in conduct which misleads the court or agency."

Despite all these high sounding comments, lawyers are famous, at least in the view of the public, for spinning the truth, for exaggerating the facts, for omitting information which conveys something less than the truth, and even for fabricating something to cover up the truth. Lawyers all too often mischaracterize the truth to win an argument, exaggerate a value to gain a perceived advantage, and misinterpret, misshape or spin the known facts and the law to further the client's goals. Shame on us!

I am reminded about the story of the journalist trying to write a major article about how different professionals think. The journalist asks the engineer, "What is 4 plus 3?" The engineer, somewhat insulted, replies, "It is 7 you idiot." The journalist writes that the engineer was quick, precise and firm in his answer. The journalist next asks the doctor the same question. The doctor replies, "I have a pretty good idea what the answer is, but I need for you to come to my office, let me conduct a complete examination and after receiving the results of lab tests, I will happily give you my diagnosis and my answer." The journalist wrote that the doctor was thorough, careful and highly professional. Then the journalist asks the lawyer, "How much is 4 plus 3?" and the lawyer immediately responds, "What do you want it to be?"

The legal profession will never be regarded by the public as moral, ethical or even professional until individual lawyers tell the truth, the whole truth and nothing but the truth, so help us God.

HONESTY: THE FOUNDATION OF PROFESSIONALISM

In late December, 2013, the American Bar Association's Standing Committee on Professionalism published *Essential Qualities of the Professional Lawyer*, Paul Haskins, Editor (*"Professional Lawyer"*). *Professional Lawyer* recognized that there is no single universally accepted definition of professionalism. Indeed, "there is no consensus on the constituent pieces of professionalism . . ." (*Professional Lawyer*, p. xxvi) We tend to define professionalism by listing the "constituent pieces" or characteristics that are found in lawyers we respect.

On April 20, 2006, the Oklahoma Bar Association's Board of Governors adopted the following definition: "Professionalism for lawyers and judges requires **honestly, integrity,** competence, civility and public service." (Emphasis added.) This definition demonstrates that personal honesty and professional integrity form the bedrock upon which professionalism rests.

While the OBA's definition of professionalism does not make specific reference to the Oklahoma Rules of Professional Conduct (5 OK Stat. Ch. 1, App. 3-A) ("Rules"), the Rules make clear that the first and highest duty of every lawyer is to be honest.

Rule 1.2(d) prohibits lawyers from assisting a client to engage in **criminal or fraudulent conduct.**

Rule 3.3 provides that a lawyer shall not: "(1) knowingly make a **false statement of fact or law** to a tribunal or **fail to correct a false statement** of material fact or law previously made to the tribunal by the lawyer; . . . or (3) offer evidence the **lawyer knows to be false . . .**"

Rule 3.4(b) provides that a lawyer shall not "**falsify evidence, counsel or assist a witness to testify falsely** . . ."

Rule 4.1 provides that a lawyer shall not knowingly "(a) make a **false statement of material fact or law to a third person; or (b) fail to disclose a material fact to a third person when disclosure is necessary to avoid assisting a criminal or fraudulent act** by a client unless disclosure is prohibited by Rule 1.6 [attorney-client privilege]."

Rule 7.1 provides in part that a "lawyer shall not make a **false or misleading communication about the lawyer or the lawyer's services. A communication is false or misleading if it contains a material misrepresentation of fact or law, or omits a fact necessary to make the communication considered as a whole not materially misleading.**"

Rule 8.1 provides that an applicant for admission to the bar shall not "(a) **knowingly make a false statement of material fact;** or (b) fail to disclose a fact necessary to correct a misapprehension . . ."

Rule 8.2 provides that a lawyer shall not "make a statement that the lawyer **knows to be false or with reckless disregard as to its truth or falsity** concerning the qualifications or integrity of a judge . . ."

Rule 8.4 states that it "is professional misconduct for a lawyer to . . . (b) commit a criminal act that reflects adversely on the lawyer's **honesty, trustworthiness or fitness as a lawyer in other respects;** (c) engage in conduct involving **dishonesty, fraud, deceit or misrepresentation** . . ." (Emphasis Added.)

It is not required that anyone rely upon the lawyer's false statements or that anyone be injured or damaged by the false statement for a <u>Rule 8.4</u> violation to occur. The statement need not even be material, essential or important in context. Read literally, a <u>Rule 8.4</u> violation occurs when the false or fraudulent or deceitful statement is made, even if no one acts on it, even if no one is hurt or damaged by it and even if the statement is not material. Comment 2 expands <u>Rule 8.4</u> further by providing that even "truthful statements that are misleading are also prohibited by this Rule."

The duty of honesty is not without exceptions. A defense counsel has no duty to disclose client confidences in a criminal case, since the client has a constitutional right not to incriminate himself. However, there is no constitutional right to remain silent or refuse to tell the truth in a civil case. There are even times when the lawyer may keep quiet and withhold information from the client, for example, when disclosure could be harmful to the client's health or welfare. (*Professional Lawyer*, p. 132-33)

Does the lawyer have a duty to correct the court when the lawyer knows that the court is acting on false facts? Yes in certain cases. The lawyer has a special duty to the court to correctly characterize his client's position, to correct statements previously made by the lawyer that are not correct, not to cite cases incorrectly and not to withhold case law in that jurisdiction which is contrary to the client's position. Disclosure is required to correct statements of fact or law made by the lawyer, even if doing so may hurt the client's position. See <u>Rule 3.3</u> (*Professional Lawyer*, p. 130). In no case is the lawyer permitted to offer false evidence or assist the client to testify falsely or assist or counsel a client to commit a crime or fraud. See <u>Rule 3.4(b)</u>. But does the lawyer in a civil case have to disclose facts contrary to the client's position when neither the court nor the opponent has asked for those facts, where the mistake does not come from the lawyer's statements?

In commercial negotiations, estimates of price or value or other similar statements not generally understood as "statements of fact" do not violate the Rule, even if the lawyer knows the statement to be false. See Comment 1 to Rule 8.4. For example, can a lawyer express an opinion that the property to be sold is worth $1 million, when the lawyer knows facts which would reduce the value to less than $500,000? Would it be acceptable if the lawyer stated that the $1 million value is his or her opinion only or is that implied? Is it an acceptable negotiation practice for the lawyer to state that "my client will take not one penny less than $1 million," when the lawyer knows that the client would readily accept less?

A further exception to the duty to tell the truth (and withhold facts necessary for the truth to be known) occurs when disclosure may conflict with the lawyer's duty of confidentiality under Rule 1.6. When the duty of confidentiality collides with the lawyer's duty of honesty under Rule 8.4, the Rules defer to the professional judgment, discretion and experience of each lawyer. There are certain times when a lawyer may disclose information received in the attorney-client relationship in order to prevent significant personal injury or financial harm or to defend claims made by the client against the lawyer. See Rule 1.6 (b)(5).

Lawyers live in a highly competitive and adversarial environment. Lawyers often face significant ethical challenges from their own clients. The lawyer often finds himself or herself in a collision between following his or her moral code and representing the client's goals, aspirations and expectations. Some clients expect their lawyer do what it takes to win, even if the lawyer has to spin, distort or even destroy the truth to do so. Clients want to win; and some clients do not care how their lawyers do it. Some clients want to win, whether or not their lawyer acts with integrity or honesty or consistent with the lawyer's internalized moral code or principles of virtue.

Acting ethically, with personal honesty and professional integrity, requires that the lawyer not just adopt an internalized moral code, but also that the lawyer act consistent with high moral principles. (*Professional Lawyer*, p. 128) There are rarely any moral absolutes. The lawyer's duty to tell the truth can often collide with the client's objectives. The lawyer's duty to tell the truth will be different in the context of a criminal case as opposed to a civil dispute. In the criminal case, the defense lawyer is not charged with a duty of truth telling, but rather there is a constitutional right of every person accused of a crime not to incriminate himself or herself. Further, the criminal trial is not a quest for the truth but is rather an opportunity for the government to prove beyond a reasonable doubt that the defendant is guilty. There is no such constitutional right against self-incrimination in a civil case, at least after the criminal charges are resolved.

Another example where a client's interest may be adverse to the lawyer's duty to disclose client secrets may occur in certain non-litigation contexts. Is there a legal or professional duty for the lawyer to disclose facts when the client refuses to make or permit the disclosure? Is the duty of disclosure determined by whether the secret is materially important? Who decides if a fact is material or not? Suppose the lawyer is asked to prepare a prospectus for a private offering of securities for a client which is insolvent. Is the lawyer required or even permitted to disclose the fact of the client's insolvency in the prospectus, if the client refuses to disclose that it is unable to pay its bills as they become due unless the offering is successfully completed? Can the lawyer help the client raise money by writing a private placement memorandum which does not disclose the client's insolvency? If the lawyer concludes that disclosure of the precarious financial condition of the client is required, can the disclosure be buried in a footnote or on the last page of a 100 page prospectus? Must the disclosure be prominent? The client's insolvency is certainly material in the context of a securities offering. I would argue that the lawyer is compelled to disclose the insolvency of the client, even over the client's vehement objection, in order to prevent a material misrepresentation and fraud upon the prospective investor. See <u>Rule 1.6</u>, which permits but does not require a lawyer to disclose the client's insolvency. See also <u>Rule 1.2</u> and <u>Rule 4.1</u>, which prohibit the lawyer from aiding or assisting the client in committing a crime or a fraud.

The lawyer's duty of honesty and integrity is not confined to the Rules of Professional Conduct. The **Lawyer's Creed** was adopted by the OBA Board of Governors on November 17, 1987 and amended on March 8, 2008. The **Lawyer's Creed** provides in part that:

(1) The lawyer will be guided by a "fundamental sense of **integrity** and fairness;" and

(2) The lawyer's word is his or her "bond."

The lawyer's duty of honesty and integrity is fleshed out further by the **Standards of Professionalism**, adopted by the OBA Board of Governors on November 20, 2002. The **Standards of Professionalism** provide in part:

1.2   In dealing with the public, "the lawyer's word should be his or her bond. We will **not knowingly misstate, distort or improperly exaggerate any fact,** opinion or legal authority and will not improperly permit our silence or inaction to mislead anyone." See also <u>1.8.</u>

<u>3.1</u>   In dealing with other lawyers, "we will be civil, courteous, respectful, **honest** and fair . . ."

<u>4.5</u>   In dealing with courts and administrative agencies, "we will never **knowingly misrepresent, mischaracterize, misquote, miscite facts or authorities, or otherwise engage in conduct which misleads the court or agency.**" (Emphasis added.)

Each one of the Rules of Professional Conduct set forth above is <u>mandatory and not permissive</u>. Violation of any of these Rules can subject the lawyer to professional discipline, including disbarment, and may even result in criminal penalties and/or civil damages. On the other hand, the **Lawyer's Creed** and the **Standards of Professionalism** are <u>permissive and not mandatory</u>. Violation of the **Lawyer's Creed** and/or the **Standards of Professionalism** cannot result in professional punishment, unless accompanied by a violation of the Rules.

The duty of a lawyer to zealously represent the client does not give the lawyer license to misrepresent facts or employ false or deceptive practices, even if intended to benefit the client. The lawyer is required to represent the client with honesty and without deceit or trickery in accordance with the law and the Rules. *(Professional Lawyer,* p. 136) See <u>Rule 8.4 (b) and (c)</u>.

The core values of personal honesty and professional integrity should not be sacrificed on the alter of a winning-at-all-costs strategy. Winning is critically important for the client and for the lawyer as well. But winning dishonestly is never worth the price. The victory is tainted for the client, and the lawyer's reputation and professional standing will be damaged beyond repair. Sacrificing fundamental beliefs of fairness, honesty, integrity and truth for the sake of a temporary success will never mean true victory. (*Professional Lawyer*, p. 15)

The *Professional Lawyer* defines each lawyer's "internalized moral code" as a deep sense of responsibility to others, especially to the client, as well as a restraint on personal self-interest. (*Professional Lawyer*, p. 9) The essence of this internal moral code is honesty, integrity and mutual respect. Embedded in this internal moral code is the Golden Rule, expressed positively as doing to others what you expect others to do to you; or expressed in the negative as not doing to others what you do not want others to do to you. The Golden Rule is a universally accepted moral standard of conduct accepted in virtually every culture throughout the history of man. You get back what you put out. Act with respect, and your opponents will respond respectfully. Act like a jerk, and you will likely get jerked around. Tell the truth, and your opponents will respond truthfully. Lie and you will never enjoy a reputation for personal or professional integrity.

Living a life based upon truth, honesty and integrity advances the client's bests interests and justifies the public's trust and confidence in the legal profession. The professional lawyer is worthy of the public's trust, because the professional lawyer's life reflects a shared value system based upon honesty, integrity and trustworthiness, a commitment to technical competence and a strong sense of service to others and to the community. (*Professional Lawyer*, p. 15)

The professional lawyer, therefore: (1) Is honest, truthful and morally upright; (2) lives by a high moral code; (3) values personal honesty and professional integrity; (4) often sacrifices personal self-interest to further the interests of the client; and (5) does what is right, even in the face of difficult or adverse personal consequences.

There is a right way to achieve every lawful goal, and there is no right way to achieve an unlawful result. In the practice of law, there are times when the lawyer must disclose facts which are adverse to the client's position, but those instances are rare. Truth is the most important and fundamental principle in lawyering. Honesty and integrity are co-equals with truth. When facing ethical challenges over issues of truth, honesty and integrity, those fundamental principles should prevail. Personal honesty and professional integrity are more than mere virtues: They are a matter of professional imperative.

SILENCING THE TRUTH: THE PENN STATE CASE

Doing the right thing is always the right thing to do. Doing the wrong thing, even for what seems to be the right reason, is never the right thing to do. Why can we not learn this simple truth?

As the scandal at Penn State University widens and unfolds, I am struck by the words of the Board of Trustee's Vice President in 2011 in announcing the dismissal of the University's President and Joe Paterno, its legendary football coach, as being "in the best interest the University." No doubt that statement is true, at least in part. But the action of the University's senior administration officials in 2002 to keep quiet about the reported rape of a 10 year old boy in the University's athletic department showers by Jerry Sandusky, a former football coach, was apparently not reported to the police, because silence was perceived then to be "in the best interest of the University." Those officials feared the University's stellar reputation for honesty and integrity would be damaged or destroyed if the alleged rape was reported.

It is now being reported that a long line of University officials, not just Mike McQueary, then a graduate student assistant foot-ball coach, head coach Joe Paterno, Vice President Gary Schultz and Athletic Director Tim Curley, but also many police and other enforcement personnel knew about the incident, but kept quiet, apparently because they wrongly believed silence was "in the best interest of the University." How could silencing the truth in this case ever be best?

When I hear the words "in the best interests of . . ." I am imme-diately put on guard: Beware of what others call "the best interest of . . ." because these words are often code words for silence, for a cover up or for spinning an explanation which omits important true facts. Half the truth is a whole lie. The road to hell is paved with good intentions. Keeping silent in the face of alleged physical harm to others, especially to a young innocent defenseless boy, is never the right thing to do, even when silence is perceived in good faith to be in the best interest of the company, the university or the government. In the alleged rape of a child, silence is always wrong.

Lawyers know that motive is important, especially in the criminal context. There are specific intent crimes that are not criminal, unless there is proof beyond a reasonable doubt of the specific intent to do them. Killing an intruder in your home is not criminal, even if you intended to shoot, if you are acting in self-defense or with the intent and purpose of protecting your family and your home. There are also general intent crimes that occur by engaging in the prohibited conduct, even if the person doing them does not know that such conduct is a crime or does not intend to do them. Intent and motive do matter, whether the issue involves criminal misconduct or moral or ethical considerations.

At least these facts seem clear. Mike McQueary reported what he saw to his father and then to his boss, Joe Paterno, who reported the alleged rape of a young boy by his long-time friend to Paterno's boss, the Athletic Director, who in turn reported the incident to his boss, the University Vice President; but no one apparently made an official report of this incident to the police. No one stopped the violence or protected the boy involved, thereby enabling potential future misconduct to occur because of the silence of those who should have acted to protect the defenseless boy and others against possible future misconduct. Apparently, each believed they were acting "for the good of and in the best interest of the University." Instead of a police report, the University's only action against Jerry Sandusky was to order him to return his keys to the University showers, which he apparently did not even do until years later. Unbelievable! The reputation, integrity and character of all those involved have now been damaged beyond repair, because they chose silence over doing the right thing. They put personal and institutional self-interest above doing what was right: protecting the boy, conducting an open and official investigation and punishing misconduct if it occurred.

This story continues to repeat itself throughout our history. The protection of self-interest at the expense of protecting the innocent who cannot protect themselves is not confined to college athletics. Many Catholic bishops and supervising Catholic Church officials have chosen not to stop the misconduct or report criminal child abuse by parish priests under their supervision "for the good of the Church." They acted out of a perverted sense of protecting the good name and reputation of the institution, rather than protecting innocent children and possible future victims. The result is that many victims have been scarred for life, and the Church has paid an enormous price in the loss of its reputation and enormous money damages because of institutional silence. Money does not heal the damages done. Payment by the Church shifts the burden to those that covered up the violence. What aggravates the Penn State scandal is that the Church scandal in Pennsylvania over priest abuse of children was on-going at the same time Jerry Sandusky was allegedly engaged in the same type of evil conduct by Church officials, yet the University officials still kept silent. Perhaps because no official action was taken as a result of the 2002 incident, the University wrongly believed that no one would find out the truth in the future. Shame on them! Where were their lawyers in this matter? Why did Church and University lawyers not require immediate disclosure?

The best interest of the University clearly was to report the facts and take appropriate action to prevent future attacks. History reveals that the truth is almost always discovered. Silence is rarely complete. Generally, there are no secrets, despite massive efforts to kept misconduct covered up. Keeping silent in the face of evil usually is not for the perceived benefit of the institution but rather for the benefit of those individuals who know the truth. Evil proliferates when good men keep quiet.

Sexual abuse of children overshadows scandals in corporate America, but the same motive that drove the Penn State officials to keep quiet drives corporate scandals too. The misconduct of senior corporate officials, choosing to look the other way when accounting misconduct is discovered or choosing to ship defective products to customers, knowing of a design defect, because not to ship those products would adversely affect the bottom line or reduce the market price for the stock, is clearly egregious. But rape of a child is unthinkable! Company officials justify their misconduct as being "in the best interest of the Company," when really they are trying to protect their own jobs and their own reputations by covering up what will surely become a public scandal anyway. Those in power always seem to believe that the truth will never be discovered. They are always wrong, even if disclosure is delayed.

Many recent public scandals and private scandals evidence a total lack of moral and ethical backbone by those who should know better, especially their lawyers. The Enron scandal and its resulting collapse is an excellent example. Creative accounting that harmed millions was covered up and misrepresented, even though senior management and their lawyers knew of the misconduct. The residential housing meltdown caused by bundling non-performing mortgages into "securitized" loan packages by highly trained professionals (some of whom were lawyers) was wrong, but no one stopped the fraud or reported the misconduct "for the good of the firm." The British Petroleum oil spill in the Gulf of Mexico was caused by sloppy engineering and an unwillingness to take necessary but expensive corrective actions and was justified by BP officials as being "in the best interest of the Company." History is replete with many other examples.

Many recent movies depict this same story of silence, wrongly justified by allegedly acting in the "best interest of an institution." Covering up misconduct rationalized as being in "best interests of an institution" always has devastating consequences for individuals affected and for the institutions involved. For example, in the movie *J. Edgar*, the first head of the FBI engaged in illegal wiretaps and blackmail of public officials in order to "protect the best interests of the country," when he really acted to protect his own personal power and position. In the movie *The General's Daughter*, an Army major general participated in the cover up of the gang rape of his daughter by West Point cadets while on maneuvers "as being in the best interest" of the Army and as facilitating the integration of more women in combat roles, when his real motive was to get another star and avoid the shame and inevitably unfavorable publicity. In the movie *Erin Brockovich*, a public utility polluted the lands around an electricity power plant, causing cancer to many local families and covered up the damage by their silence, purportedly acting "in the best interest of the company." In the movie *Class Action*, an automobile manufacturer covered up the design defect in a vehicle's faulty left rear turn signal, knowing that the defect would ultimately cause explosions in a small number of cases but estimating that the damages would likely cost less than fixing the design defect, thereby protecting the bottom line and acting in the "best interest of the company." These are just a few of many examples of the same corrupt analysis: Silence in the name of "the best interest of" the country, the Army, a public university or a company always has devastating results, because silence about misconduct is simply wrong. Keeping silent in the face of wrong, especially when perpetrated against a young boy, is always wrong!

Choosing or failing to do the right thing always has unintended consequences. Failing to do the right thing, because it is inconvenient or may damage personal or institutional reputations or reduce the bottom line will always have larger, more adverse consequences than if the right thing had been done in the first place. Covering up the failure to do the right thing will always prove more devastating when the true facts are discovered. And in our world where the public's unquenchable thirst for scandal exists, the true facts will be discovered. Once blood is in the water, the sharks will gather for the kill.

But doing the right thing solely for fear of being discovered is not the right reason to do the right thing. It is said that integrity is doing the right thing when no one is watching and getting caught is unlikely. Reporting the possible rape of a child is required, not because you fear that you will get caught by not reporting. Instead, reporting this misconduct is the right action to take, simply because it is the right thing to do. Period!

Lawyers are often asked to give advice to clients faced with difficult moral and ethical decisions. Lawyers are ethically and morally prohibited from participating with clients who engage in criminal misconduct (see, for example, Rule 1.16(b) and Rule 8.4), and lawyers become participants in their misconduct when they counsel them to engage in misconduct and/or help them cover it up, unless silence is required by the attorney-client privilege (See Rule 1.6). The attorney-client privilege varies from state-to-state but would not generally protect speech by a client to counsel involving future criminal activity, especially where serious personal injury is likely to occur. I believe the Rules and good moral judgment require the lawyer to report the facts to enforcement agencies, even if the client objects. Lawyers should always encourage clients to do the right thing for the right reasons, even though doing the right thing is often both inconvenient and potentially harmful to them. Doing the right thing for the right reason will always prove to be right and wise.

There is no right way to do a wrong thing. Doing the wrong thing, even when the reason for doing so seems to support a higher purpose, is still doing the wrong thing. Covering up the misconduct "for the good of the company" is not righteous or praiseworthy, but is instead wrongful and contemptible. The story of the Good Samaritan teaches this lesson. The priest and the Levite walked on by, because helping would be inconvenient and cost them time and money. Helping was the right thing to do, but only the Samaritan stopped to help. A lifetime of good conduct can be destroyed in an instant of silence, when action is required to help another. Coach Paterno's lifetime of achievements has been sullied by his momentary lapse in judgment, even if his motive was to help his long-time friend and his University avoid a scandal.

When someone justifies a particular action with the comment that the action was taken "in the best interest of the institution," beware! The proper action is to do the right thing, not to protect reputation or image or standing. Instead, do what is right for the right reasons, and counsel your clients to do so too. Doing right is always the right thing to do, even if it is inconvenient or expensive or embarrassing or creates uncertainty or is unpopular or is opposed by the personal interests of friends and colleagues. Doing right will justify itself. Doing what is wrong will always be wrong, even if the reasons are thought to be wholesome or praiseworthy.

Lawyers are uniquely positioned to help avoid the greater evil by counselling our clients to do the right thing. Lawyers become part of the problem when we fail to do the right thing.

CIVILITY: THE CORNERSTONE OF PROFESSIONALISM

In late December, 2013, the American Bar Association's Standing Committee on Professionalism published *Essential Qualities of the Professional Lawyer ("Professional Lawyer")*. Two of the 20 chapters are devoted to civility. Chapter 3 is entitled "Civility is the Core of Professionalism," and Chapter 4 is entitled "The Practical Case for Civility." *Professional Lawyer* calls civility the "cornerstone of professionalism." (*Professional Lawyer,* p. 35)

"Civility" means treating others fairly and with respect, courtesy and decency. "Civility" means not being rude, offensive, insulting, vulgar, coercive, overly confrontational, abusive, abrasive, humiliating, harassing or disruptive.

Civility compels lawyers to show respect to their adversaries, to the courts and to the public. Civility toward an adversary does not mean agreement with the opponent's position. Resolving disagreements is the business of the legal profession. But disagreement does not have to be disagreeable. Problem-solving is best achieved by adversaries treating their opponents with respect, rather than by using bully tactics. Professional lawyers take exception to positions, without attacking the persons who express those positions.

Civility as a code of conduct is concisely expressed by the Golden Rule, a universally accepted moral code of conduct for all people in virtually every culture throughout the history of man: Do to others what you expect others to do to you; and do not do to others what you do not want others to do to you. Act with respect, and your opponents will respond respectfully. Tell the truth, and your opponents will respond truthfully. To paraphrase Lao Tzu, treat those who respect you with respect, and treat those with respect who do not respect you. In this way, respect is established. On the other hand, you get back what you put out. Act like a jerk, and you will likely get jerked around. Lie and you will never enjoy a reputation for personal or professional integrity.

You may not like your opponent, and you may disagree vehemently with the positions your opponent takes, but that does not give you license to be rude or offensive or to attack them personally. Professional lawyers take exception to positions without attacking the persons who express those positions. (*Professional Lawyer*, p. 36)

Civility is not a onetime event. Civility is a lifetime code of conduct. The professional lawyer: (1) models respect for clients, adversaries, courts and the public; (2) demonstrates courtesy to others; (3) avoids harassment, intimidation and insults; (4) never attacks opponents personally; (5) is not a bully; (6) does not employ take-no-prisoner tactics; and (6) disagrees without being disagreeable.

Even though civility is the cornerstone of professionalism, the word "civility" does not appear in any of the Oklahoma Rules of Professional Conduct. 5 OK Stat. Ch.1 3-A ("Rules"). Being nice, courteous and respectful is not compelled by the Rules, and being inconsiderate, unkind or disrespectful is not professionally punishable by the Rules. Conduct that is rude, offensive, insulting, humiliating or sarcastic is also not prohibited by the Rule. However, Rule 3.5(3) prohibits a lawyer from communicating with a juror "if the communication involves misrepresentation, coercion, duress or harassment;" and Rule 4.4(a) provides that a lawyer shall not engage in conduct "for no substantial purpose other than to embarrass, delay or burden a third person ..." It is not even a violation of the Rules to be mean or to act like a jerk. A lawyer cannot be disbarred or professionally punished just because the lawyer is rude or disagreeable or disrespectful. Even so, civility forms the foundation upon which professionalism rests; and civility is inherent in and is actually the essence of most of the Rules. Treating others as you want to be treated by others is the commandment upon which all the laws and the prophets are based.

The OBA Board of Governors has for some time been focused on civility as an integral and essential part of professionalism. On November 17, 1989, the OBA Board of Governors adopted the **Lawyer's Creed**, which focuses almost exclusively on *civility*. See www.okbar.org/members/ethicscounsel/lawyerscreed. The **Lawyer's Creed** states that:

(1) The lawyer will be guided by a "fundamental sense of fair play;"

(2) The lawyer will not abuse the system or act in an arbitrary manner;

(3) The lawyer will not harass or bully by delay;

(4) The lawyer will act with "decency and courtesy;"

(5) The lawyer will be punctual and respect the time commitments of others;

(6) The lawyer will cooperate with opposing counsel;

(7) The lawyer will not employ offensive or "rude behavior;" and

(8) The lawyer will "act with *civility*."

On November 20, 2002, the OBA Board of Governors adopted the **Standards of Professionalism**. The full text of the **Standards** can be found at www.okbar.org/members/ethicscounsel/standards-professionalism. These **Standards** contain an extensive list of specific examples of civility, especially in the context of litigated matters, as follows:

1.2   In dealing with the public, the lawyer will be "honest, professional and civil."

1.10   In dealing with the public, the lawyer will not "engender bias" by reason of a "person's race, color, national origin, ethnicity, religion, gender, sexual orientation or disability."

2.6   In dealing with clients, the lawyer will not "engage in abusive or offensive conduct."

2.7   In dealing with clients, the lawyer will not be "uncivil, rude, abrasive, abusive, vulgar, antagonistic, obstructive or obnoxious."

3.1(a) In dealing with opposing counsel, the lawyer will be "civil, courteous, respectful, honest and fair."

3.2.(a) In discovery, the lawyer will not use "scheduling to harass counsel or generate needless expenses." See also 3.2(b) (2).

3.2(b) (1) In depositions, the lawyer will be accommodating in scheduling matters.

3.2(b) (6) In depositions, the lawyer will not "abuse others or indulge in offensive conduct directed to other counsel, parties or witnesses" and will "refrain from disparaging personal remarks or acrimony toward" others. See also 3.2(b) (13).

3.2(c) (1) In document requests, the lawyer will not make requests to "annoy, embarrass or harass a party."

3.3(a) In scheduling, the lawyer will act with "civility and courtesy."

3.3(c) In scheduling, the lawyer will not withhold consent unreasonably.

3.4(b) In scheduling, the lawyer will agree to reasonable requests for extensions.

3.4(c) In scheduling, the lawyer will agree "as a matter of courtesy to the first request for extension."

3.6(a) In dealing with non-parties, the lawyer will be "civil, courteous and professional."

3.6(b) In dealing with non-parties, the lawyer will "not annoy, humiliate, intimidate or harass the individual."

3.6(b) In business transactions, the lawyer will "mark all requested changes and revisions."

4.1 In dealing with courts, the lawyer will "speak and write civilly and respectfully."

4.4 In dealing with courts, the lawyer will "not bring disorder or disruption to a proceeding."

<u>4.5</u>   In dealing with courts, the lawyer will "never knowingly misrepresent, mischaracterize, misquote, or miscite facts or authorities."

<u>4.8</u>   In dealing with the court's staff, the lawyer will speak civilly and respectfully.

<u>4.9</u>   In written materials submitted to the court, the lawyer will be "factual and concise, accurately state current law, and fairly represent the party's position without unfairly attacking the opposing party or opposing counsel."

<u>4.9 (d)</u> In written materials submitted to the court, the lawyer will "avoid disparaging the intelligence, ethics, morals, integrity, or personal behavior of the opposing party, counsel or witness."

While the **Lawyer's Creed** and the **Standards of Professionalism** are not specifically written into the Rules of Professional Conduct, they represent conduct which lawyers <u>should</u> achieve, rather than the minimal conduct which lawyers <u>must</u> demonstrate as required by the Rules.

On April 20, 2006, the Board of Governors of the Oklahoma Bar Association adopted the following definition: "Professionalism for lawyers and judges requires honestly, integrity, competence, **civility** and public service." (Emphasis added.) Civility is inherent in and an essential part of professionalism in the legal profession.

Almost from the earliest days of law school, lawyers are taught to be zealous advocates for their clients. Indeed, the Preamble to the Rules states that a lawyer is to be a zealous advocate for the client.

Interestingly, the word "zealous" does not appear in any of the Rules. There is a natural tension between being a zealous advocate, on the one hand, and being a civil, courteous and respectful lawyer, on the other hand. However, zealous advocacy does not mean the lawyer must become a zealot for the client. The duty of zealous advocacy does not give the lawyer a license to be unprofessional, uncivil or uncooperative.

Some lawyers believe that treating the opponent with courtesy and respect is a sign of weakness. The opposite is actually true. Contrary to popular belief, the empirical data demonstrate that the client's interests are far better served when the lawyer acts with respect and civility, as opposed to when the lawyer is rude or abrasive or offensive. (*Professional Lawyer*, p. 46) Incivility usually backfires. Being confrontational costs more money and takes more time than being civil. Judges tend to side with the lawyer who respects others. Clients do not like lawyers who are rude or offensive. (*Professional Lawyer*, p. 51-53) **"Very often the best way forward for even the most egotistical, self-interested and self-absorbed lawyer and their egotistical, self-interested and self-absorbed clients is through, rather than around, civility."** (*Professional Lawyer*, p. 51)

ZEALOUS ADVOCACY: A DUTY WITH LIMITS

The Preamble to the Oklahoma Rules of Professional Conduct (5 OK Stat. Ch. 1, App. 3-A) ("Rules") states that a lawyer is "a representative of clients, an officer of the legal system, and a public citizen having special responsibility for the quality of justice." In discharging the lawyer's duty to the client, the lawyer is: (1) an advisor; (2) an instructor; (3) an advocate; (4) a negotiator and (5) an evaluator. The lawyer's duty as an advocate all too often overshadows the lawyer's other roles and duties.

The Rule of Law is premised upon a long history and tradition that the best way to uncover the truth and to insure procedural fairness and substantive justice is for opposing sides to be represented by zealous advocates, each pursuing with passion the interests of his or her respective clients. See ABA Cannons of Professional Ethics, 1908. The Preamble to the Rules provides that:

"As an advocate, the lawyer **zealously asserts** the client's position **under the rules of the adversary system** . . . Within the framework of the Rules, however, many difficult issues of professional discretion can arise. Such issues must be resolved through the **exercise of sensitive professional and moral judgment** guided by the basic principles underlying the Rules. These principles include the lawyer's obligation **zealously to protect and pursue a client's legitimate interests, within the bounds of the law, while maintaining a professional, courteous and civil attitude toward all persons involved in the legal system.**" (Emphasis added.)

<u>Rule 1.3</u> requires that a lawyer act with "reasonable diligence and promptness in representing a client." Comment 1 to <u>Rule 1.3</u> provides that a lawyer "must act with commitment and dedication to the interests of the client and with **zeal in advocacy** upon the client's behalf." To the surprise of most lawyers, no Rule in Oklahoma requires zeal or zealous advocacy, and no Comment to any Oklahoma Rule (other than Comment 1 to <u>Rule 1.3</u>) uses the words "zeal" or "zealous" or "zealously" to describe the lawyer's ethical duties and responsibilities. Even so, most lawyers believe that they are required to act zealously on behalf of the client.

Zeal is defined many ways, such as: (1) great enthusiasm and energy in pursuit of a person or a cause; (2) fervent devotion to an objective or a belief system; (3) tireless devotion to a cause; (4) timely action in compliance with an objective; and (5) prompt willingness in support of a position or belief. Synonyms for zeal include ardor, passion, fervor, zest, eagerness and readiness. Antonyms for zeal include indifference, apathy, passivity, stoicism and unresponsiveness. See WordNet 3.0, Princeton University

Zeal does not encompass excessive advocacy, radical unsupported positions or outrageous extremism in the lawyer's articulation of the client's position. Many lawyers, however, distort this duty of zealousness by seeking to justify extreme positions and outrageous conduct in the name of "zealous advocacy." All too often, lawyers take positions in the name of "zealous" representation which they assert are literally legal but which they know will create materially false impressions. They assert that the end justifies the means and that winning is everything, even if in winning they lie, cheat or spin the truth to win. They claim that what is true depends upon the circumstances, what is right depends upon cultural or political attitudes and what is wise depends upon the client's position or the jury's verdict.

I believe that it is entirely proper for a zealous advocate to: (1) question the truth without being dishonest; (2) test the testimony without obfuscating the truth; (3) attack positions without attacking persons; (4) pursue with passion and diligence the client's position within the legal system; (5) test the boundaries of the law; and (6) seek to win without being disrespectful or discourteous.

I assert, however, that acting with zeal does not warrant dishonesty or disrespect and never justifies extreme or outrageous positions or conduct. Zeal does not require the lawyer to become a zealot for the client. I also assert that what is true is true, no matter who says it; what is right is right, no matter who claims otherwise; and what is wise depends upon immutable time-honored moral principles, including mutual respect, civility and the Golden Rule.

I assert further that it is not only possible, but it is professionally necessary, that lawyers pursue their client's objectives zealously but that they do so within the rules of law and with honesty, integrity and respect. I also assert that:

Lawyers can be zealous without being rude, offensive or abrasive.

Lawyers can be zealous without being discourteous, disrespectful or dishonest.

Lawyers can be zealous without misrepresentations, mischaracterizations or distorted citations of the law.

Lawyers can be zealous without being abusive, intimidating or vulgar.

Lawyers can be zealous without humiliating, embarrassing or attacking their opponent.

Lawyers can be zealous without giving half-answers, hiding the truth or recklessly disregarding the facts or the truth.

Lawyers can be zealous without cheating, lying or tricking their opponent.

Lawyers can be zealous without being sleazy, obnoxious or being a jerk.

Lawyers can be zealous without uncivilized, unprincipled or immoral conduct.

Lawyers can be zealous by disagreeing without being disagreeable.

Lawyers can be zealous without abandoning core professional values of truth, honesty, integrity and mutual respect.

While the Preamble to the Rules requires lawyers to be zealous advocates for their client's positions, the Preamble also states that the basic principles underlying the Rules include "**the lawyer's obligation zealously to protect and pursue the client's legitimate interests, <u>within the bounds of law</u>, while maintaining a professional, courteous and civil attitude toward all persons involved in the legal system.**" (Emphasis added.)

It is important that lawyers not only espouse high principles of truth, respect, civility and professionalism, but also that they live them out. There should be no difference between what lawyers should say or do and what lawyers actually say and do. There should be no difference between the rules which should govern the lawyer's conduct and what the lawyer's conduct actually is. There should be no difference between what lawyers pray on Sunday and what lawyers do on Monday.

Following the letter of the law is not sufficient if a proposed course of conduct is morally reprehensible, insulting, disrespectful or dishonest. Even if a proposed action or position is literally legal, that does not mean it is right, appropriate, moral or justifiable. It is not enough for lawyers to ask: Is the client's position legal? It is also necessary that lawyers ask: Is it respectful? Is it fair? Is it right?

The legal profession cannot justify its special responsibility for the quality of justice or for society's adherence to the Rule of Law, unless each lawyer individually and the profession as a whole act within the bounds of law and civility. As guardians of the Rule of Law, lawyers must accept the responsibility zealously to represent their clients while, at the same time, zealously act within the bounds of the law, decency and mutual respect.

Professionalism is a life style which internalizes the Golden Rule. Civility is an essential part of the lawyer's life. Lawyers are expected to be men and women of high moral character, technical proficiency and respectful conduct. Lawyers who embrace civility toward their opponents do so, not just because it is the right way to act, but also because it is the most effective and efficient way to succeed. Zealous advocacy within the framework of the law is an important duty. Civility and mutual respect are part of the framework of the law, are in the best interests of the lawyers and their clients and are a necessary imperative for the furtherance of the Rule of Law.

LIVING PROFESSIONALLY

Lawyers are licensed as professionals by each state in order to assist their clients to help resolve legal disputes and conflicts. Lawyers are judged by others by what they do, not by what they think or say or believe. Doing is more important than saying, knowing or believing. The Good Samaritan stopped to help, while the priest and the Levite passed by the one in need. Our actions speak louder than our words. Here are some suggestions which will help you be a professional role model for others:

A. **Know What is Right**. The first challenge in acting ethically is knowing what is right. In most situations, we do not have to look very far to identify the right thing to do. Most of us know instinctively that lying, cheating, stealing and hurting others are actions which simply are not "right." Similarly, we also know that telling the truth, acting with integrity and helping others in need are the "right" things to do. We know these things because of: (1) our conscience, (2) the laws, (3) our customs, (4) our role models and (5) our faith. For me, if my dad would not approve it, I knew that I should not do it. Knowing what is right is the first step in doing what is right.

B. **Do What is Right.** Knowing what is right is generally not our problem. Doing what we know is right is sometimes much harder than knowing what is right. Lawyers are advocates for the interests of their clients, and there will be times when the client's desires will not meet our smell test for doing the right thing. While the client sets the goals and objectives, it is the lawyer that is responsible for how those goals are accomplished. The client cannot require the lawyer to violate the law, even in an effort to achieve the client's objectives. Likewise, the client cannot require the lawyer to violate the Rules of Professional Conduct, even if doing so would give a perceived advantage to the client. One way for the wrong to prevail is for good people to do nothing to stop it. Silence in the face of wrong nourishes evil. There is no right way to do the wrong thing. Doing a wrong thing, even to achieve a right result, is still doing the wrong thing.

We usually get back what we give out. Acting with mutual respect for others generally achieves more effective results than not being courteous and professional. Reacting with too much emotion and desiring to win at all cost are just two characteristics which sometimes cause lawyers, their staff and others to do what they know to be wrong. Before taking a questionable course of action, ask the following questions:

(1) Is the proposed action the right thing to do?

(2) Is the proposed action legal?

(3) Is the proposed action honest?

(4) Will the people I respect most approve if I do it?

(5) Will I be proud to have done it?

(6) Is there a more effective way to accomplish my goal?

C. **Deciding Between Good Alternatives.** Generally, there is more than one way to achieve a desired result, each of which is lawful and each of which may be "good" and "beneficial" and "right," at least to some extent. These situations require that we choose the best from among the good alternatives, that is, "chose the best from the rest." When multiple good alternatives exist, deciding which course of action to follow is often difficult, especially when the likely consequences are uncertain. Discussing those alternatives in advance with your client is important. If possible, get the client to "buy in" to your proposed course of action, thereby avoiding later second guessing by the client. Ultimately, your judgment, common sense, experience, training, conscience and intuition will be your best guides when deciding the best alternative from among competing good alternatives. You should be guided by the following principles:

(1) Be true to the truth.

(2) Follow the spirit of the law, not just the letter of the law.

(3) Do the most good and the least harm.

(4) Respect the rights and interests of your client and others.

(5) Be true to yourself.

(6) Act with decency and courtesy toward others.

D. **Focus on Living Ethically.** It is important to know that being an "ethical lawyer" does not just mean following a set of laws, rules, regulations, codes or standards. Instead, professionalism for the lawyer requires living an ethical life, not just talking about it. We must walk the talk, not just talk the talk. Everything we say, everything we write and everything we do involves making the "right" choice for the "right" reason at the "right." time. To that end, the following principles are guides to assist you in living the professional life:

(1) Say what you mean, and do what you say.

(2) Act as if your father or mother or mentor, or better yet God, is watching. He is.

(3) Do what is "right," even when no one is watching and even if what you do will never be discovered or made public.

(4) Be truthful in all statements.

(5) Respect the rights and interests of others.

(6) Do more than is expected of you.

(7) Practice poise and patience.

(8) Do your best in all you do. Good enough is not good enough.

(9) Do to others what you would want others to do to you.

(10) Give quality time and your best effort to your clients.

(11) Make truth, honesty, integrity and mutual respect for others core values which you embrace and by which you live.

(12) Celebrate integrity. Reject dishonesty and deceitfulness.

(13) Be an ethical role model for others. Others are watching you for guidance.

(14) Make a difference, not just a living.

(15) Become part of the solution, not part of the problem.

(16) Serve your clients, but also serve justice and the rule of law.

(17) Be an instrument for positive change.

(18) Be yourself, not what you think others want you to be.

(19) Be a solution-seeker, not a boulder in the way of solving problems.

(20) Be a problem-solver, not one who perpetuates the problem.

(21) Be a peace-maker, not a trouble-maker.

The Book of Proverbs in the Bible was written primarily by Solomon, who is regarded by many as the wisest and perhaps the richest man who ever lived. Proverbs contains more than 3,000 practical guides for ethical conduct. Most of them are just as useful today as in Solomon's time. Proverbs urges man to achieve significance beyond success by acting with wisdom beyond personal pride or wealth. Professionalism requires each lawyer to live a life that reflects honesty, integrity, character, civility and service. Embrace what is right. Do what is wise. Model honesty and mutual respect for others. By living a professional life, you will make a difference.

TOP TEN PROFESSIONALISM TIPS

The April, 2010 Your ABA Newsletter announced a new ABA book entitled "*The Busy Lawyer's Guide to Success*" by Reid F. Trautz and Dan Pinnington. The book lists 10 things that lawyers do which most annoy their clients:

1. Not returning phone calls

2. Making clients wait in the reception area

3. Lack of civility and respect towards others

4. Name dropping

5. Not explaining legal jargon

6. Not meeting promised deadlines

7. Not delivering a promised result

8. Not communicating for long periods

9. Not being prepared

10. Sending a large invoice without warning or explanation

Lawyers can eliminate these most annoying complaints and avoid meritorious grievances by embracing and following the core values of professionalism: Honesty, integrity, competence, civility and service. The following are my top ten tips for practicing professionalism:

1. **Be Honest in ALL Things.**

Make your word be your bond.

Your clients expect it.

Your adversaries desire it.

Your judge depends upon it.

The Rules of Professional Conduct require it.

The Rule of Law is built upon it.

2. **Be an Effective Communicator.**

Get an engagement letter.

Agree upon the scope of your work.

Explain how your fees are determined.

List what expenses are to be reimbursed by the client.

Listen carefully to your client's questions, concerns and complaints.

Explain legal jargon. Make sure your client understands.

If your client does not understand, explain again until the client does.

Seek your client's "buy in" to your tactics and strategy.

Keep your client promptly informed.

3. **Be Competent**.

Get prepared.

Learn the facts that support your client's position.

Learn the facts that do not support your client's position.

Determine how to prove the facts needed to establish your client's position.

The provable facts generally control the result.

Understand applicable laws, rules and regulations.

Determine what interests are behind your client's goals.

Determine what interests are behind your opponent's positions and demands.

Work faithfully but fairly to achieve the client's lawful objectives.

Do not promise any specific result. Promise your best efforts.

4. **<u>Be Respectful.</u>**

Treat others with respect.

Do to others what you expect them to do to you.

Do not do to others what you do not want done to you.

You get back what you dish out.

Do not retaliate to personal attacks.

Be on time.

Do not contest what is not in dispute.

Agree on insignificant facts and issues.

Dispute only significant, substantive issues.

Compromise nominal issues to obtain substantive success.

5. **<u>Be Responsive.</u>**

Return your client's phone calls promptly.

Respond to your client's emails promptly.

Answer your client's questions thoroughly.

Copy your client on all correspondence and filings.

Keep your client timely informed.

6. **<u>Be Responsible.</u>**

Evaluate your client's objectives honestly.

Be realistic in assessing your client's goals and objectives.

Provide your client with independent and impartial advice.

Do not exaggerate your client's chances of success.

Evaluate honestly your opponent's chances of success.

Do not promise your client victory but promise your best efforts.

Do what you say when you say.

Do not promise unrealistic deadlines.

Meet deadlines promised or explain why.

Coordinate and communicate with the client effectively.

7. **<u>Be a Problem-Solver.</u>**

Look for solutions, not disputes or delays.

Reduce emotional reactions.

Seek agreement on shared interests.

Avoid taking hard legal positions.

Compromise the insignificant to achieve substantive success.

Evaluate carefully all options and alternative solutions.

Be creative in furthering your client's goals and interests.

8. **Be Available.**

Make time for your client.

Establish parameters for your availability.

Be flexible to meet your client's circumstances.

Be reasonable and accommodating in respecting the client's needs.

A great lawyer that is not available is not useful to the client.

9. **Be Civil.**

Treat your opponents with respect and courtesy.

Cooperate with your opponent in scheduling.

Act with fundamental fairness.

Eliminate rude, abusive and insensitive language and conduct.

Avoid humiliating, harassing and embarrassing comments.

Do not engage in name calling.

Attack positions, not people.

Attack principles, not people.

Eliminate Rambo, bullying, take-no-prisoner tactics.

10. **Be a Peace-Maker.**

Seek the truth.

Speak the truth.

Do not spin the truth.

Do not withhold the truth.

Identify common interests of the client and the opponent.

Work to achieve win-win solutions based upon common interests.

Eliminate fire words.

Minimize emotional discord.

Press for peaceful solutions.

Be an instrument of peace.

Lawyers play a variety of vital roles for their clients, including being the client's advisor, teacher, advocate, negotiator, conciliator, mediator, problem-solver and representative. But lawyers are also officers of the court, public citizens and indispensable participants in furtherance of the Rule of Law. Being a lawyer is a privilege, not a right. That privilege carries with it the responsibility to act in a professional, courteous and respectful manner.

When one lawyer fails to act with professionalism, the entire legal profession suffers. Lawyers who practice professionalism are more effective, more efficient, more successful and more respected than those who do not. When we act like professionals, the clients will benefit, the legal system will be more respected and the Rule of Law will be enhanced. We owe our clients our best efforts, and that means we will pursue their goals with professionalism.

ABC'S OF PROFESSIONALISM

Life in the practice of law is not easy and does not always result in victory for the client or for the lawyer. Being a "professional" and acting with "professionalism" requires that the lawyer's business life, professional life and personal life embrace and reflect common principles of honesty, integrity and civility. Without these, life as a professional is not possible.

On April 20, 2008, the <u>Tulsa World</u> published an editorial by Harvey MacKay, one of America's best known motivational speakers, entitled *"The ABC's of Better Business."* The ABC's are the building blocks of language, and they are essential elements of all our communications.

The following are some suggestions for the ABC's of Professionalism:

ATTITUDE is a choice. Choose to care.

BELIEVE that truth and right will prevail over falsehood and evil.

COMPETENCE is not possible without character.

DEDICATE yourself to achieving your client's goals within the bounds of the law.

EXPERIENCE enhances competence. Experience develops instinct and sound judgment.

FORTITUDE fosters faith in the rule of law and in the system of equal justice for all.

GRATITUDE is for the opportunity to assist clients solve their legal problems.

HONESTY is the first duty of every lawyer.

INTEGRITY requires character, without which a lawyer is just a hired gun.

JUSTICE follows sound judgment, honest effort and the pursuit of the truth.

KNOWLEDGE is a critical element of competence. Use knowledge and experience to produce wise independent judgment.

LISTEN to learn what interests are behind your client's positions.

MEANING and purpose are achieved through service to others.

NECESSITY speaks the truth and does what is right.

OVERCOMING obstacles requires your best efforts.

PERCEPTION is not always the truth. Pursue the truth, not perception.

QUALITY requires competence, commitment, skill and judgment.

RIGHT results are based upon truth and moral integrity.

SERVICE to others is a fundamentals principle upon which the legal profession rests.

TRUTH and honesty are fundamental duties of every lawyer.

UNDERSTANDING the facts and the law is essential to success.

VIRTUE lived out always leads to victory.

WINNING occurs when truth, honesty, integrity and wisdom collide.

XPERTISE is achieved by hard work, experience and sound judgment.

YOU will make a difference if you do what is right and you do your best.

ZEALOUS advocacy means enthusiastic support for your client's goals within the bounds of the law. Zealous advocacy does not require or permit you to be a zealot for your client.

There are many other ways to define the building blocks of the legal professionalism. Experience demonstrates that lawyers who embrace professionalism make a positive difference for their clients and for the legal profession as a whole. Respect and admiration follow the lawyer who embraces the principles of professionalism, not only because that is the right thing to do, but also because following the ABCs of professionalism produces successful results.

THE GRIEVANCE PROCESS

Lawyers are the brunt of numerous degrading jokes, some of which are really funny, at least on the surface. Personal injury lawyers in particular are much maligned, especially in the face of publicity involving a significant recovery in an automobile accident. One recent comment expressed an all too often public sentiment:

"Lawyers representing two orphaned children in a tragic automobile accident got more than each child did individually. The lawyers do not have a license just to practice law; they have a license to steal. Lawyers are overpaid and are simply legalized thieves."

The comment came in a case involving a structured settlement in which each of the two children orphaned as a result of the accident received an initial cash payment of $250,000 each and the balance of $1,250,000 each to be paid later, while the lawyers were awarded 40% of the total settlement, or $2,000,000. While these cases are rare, the public seems to believe that all lawyers are "overpaid" and are "legalized thieves."

There is no doubt that the legal profession needs to do a better job in promoting public awareness of the high standards of professionalism required of those who practice law. All persons who wish to practice law in Oklahoma must obtain a license from the Oklahoma Supreme Court. Under current law, each applicant must have received a bachelor's degree and a law degree, must have passed a three day bar examination and must demonstrate good moral character. See 5 OK Stat. Section 12. Each lawyer must take an oath to comply with the law, including the Rules of Professional Conduct ("Rules"). See 5 OK Stat. Section 2

The Rules were promulgated by and are administered by the Oklahoma Supreme Court. The Rules establish minimum standards of professional conduct required of each lawyer in Oklahoma. The Preamble to the Rules recognizes the special and unique role played by lawyers in our free society. "A lawyer is a representative of clients, an officer of the legal system and a public citizen having special responsibility for the quality of justice." The lawyer is also an advocate, an advisor, a counselor, a negotiator, a mediator, an evaluator and an intermediary for and on behalf of the client in the resolution of disputes. These roles sometimes conflict, requiring the lawyer to act with special care, prudence, experienced judgment, good common sense and wisdom.

The Preamble also recognizes that allegations of professional misconduct can be abused and subvert the legitimate purpose of self-regulation. Consequently, the Preamble makes clear that the Rules do not give rise to a private cause of action; and violation of a Rule does not "create a presumption that a legal duty has been breached. The Rules are designed to provide guidance to lawyers . . . [and] are not designed to be a basis for civil liability."

While the courts are open to litigate allegations of negligence by lawyers, only the Oklahoma Supreme Court can impose professional punishment upon an Oklahoma lawyer for violating the Rules. In most instances, claims of "legal malpractice" involve allegations of negligence which may not be violations of the Rules. Likewise, fee disputes generally do not give rise to a violation of the Rules.

To enhance public confidence in the integrity of the legal profession, enforcement of the Rules requires reasonable access by the public to bring complaints of alleged professional misconduct against a lawyer to the attention of the profession. On the other hand, the lawyer against whom claims of professional misconduct are made must be afforded a fair and independent opportunity to respond to allegations of misconduct.

To that end, the Court has adopted Rules Governing Disciplinary Proceedings. 5 OK Stat. Ch.1—App. 1-A ("DP Rules"). The Court has established a Professional Responsibility Commission ("PRC") which consists of 7 members, 5 of whom are lawyers appointed to 3 year terms by the President of the Oklahoma Bar Association and 2 of whom are not lawyers; one is appointed by the Speaker of the Oklahoma House of Representatives and one is appointed by the President Pro Tempore of the Oklahoma Senate. The members of the PRC serve without compensation.

The Court has delegated to the General Counsel ("GC") of the Oklahoma Bar Association ("OK Bar") the duty to investigate and prosecute before the Oklahoma Supreme Court allegations of professional misconduct. See DP Rule 3.2. Every month, the GC's office presents to the PRC its recommendations for disposition of grievances which have been filed with its office and which have been investigated for factual accuracy and legal sufficiency.

The PRC meets monthly to consider grievances filed against Oklahoma lawyers, as presented by the GC. The PRC either determines to dismiss the grievance or directs that a formal complaint be filed against the lawyer. See DP Rule 2 et seq.

If the PRC determines that a formal complaint should be filed against a lawyer, the GC's office prosecutes that complaint before the Professional Responsibility Tribunal ("Tribunal"). See DP Rule 4 et seq. The Tribunal consists of 7 panels, each consisting of 2 lawyers and 1 lay person. The 14 lawyers are appointed by the President of the Oklahoma Bar, and the 7 lay persons are appointed by the Governor of the State of Oklahoma. If a Tribunal panel recommends discipline, after a hearing on the merits in which the lawyer has a right to appear and present arguments against the allegations, the GC's office prosecutes the case before the Oklahoma Supreme Court.

Approximately 1,700 grievances are filed with the GC's office annually. All of these grievances are checked for factual and legal sufficiency by the full-time paid staff of the GC's office. All of these grievances are evaluated against the Rules. The complaining party has an opportunity to present in writing the facts which gave rise to the grievance. The attorney has an opportunity to present in writing the attorney's response. All submissions are confidential and are required to be in writing. No hearing is held, unless the PRC requires that a formal grievance be filed.

AVOIDING A GRIEVANCE

Malcolm Gladwell's 2006 national bestseller, *"Blink,"* contains a fascinating discussion about the reasons why surgeons get sued for medical malpractice. Gladwell reports that patients file lawsuits against their doctors, when the patients "were rushed or ignored or treated poorly." *Blink* at 40. The same can generally be said about grievance allegations filed against lawyers.

While acting as Chair of the TCBA Professional Responsibility Committee for several years and being on the Committee for many more years, I have been involved in evaluating several hundred grievances filed against Oklahoma lawyers. Most grievances result from clients who feel ignored, misinformed or disrespected. Virtually every grievance contains allegations that the lawyer: (1) did not return phone calls; (2) did not keep the client informed; (3) did not charge a fair fee; and (4) did not treat the client with respect. Many of the client's frustrations come from the lawyer's failure to communicate effectively with the client.

Lawyers cannot prevent a disgruntled or dissatisfied client from filing a grievance with no basis in fact or law, but lawyers can take simple steps to avoid their client's frustrations and their own violations of the Rules of Professional Conduct. Here are some practical suggestions:

<u>Get a Written Engagement Agreement.</u> The failure of the lawyer to explain clearly to the client the scope of the engagement and the way fees and expenses will be charged are frequent causes for grievances. Grievances and fee disputes often occur when the client does not understand the scope of the engagement, does not understand how the lawyer computes the fee and does not understand what expenses are expected to be reimbursed. While written engagement agreements are not required by the Oklahoma Rules of Professional Conduct ("Rules"), except in contingent fee cases (See Rule 1.5), written engagement agreements are always helpful in resolving fee disputes and potential grievances.

(1) The scope of the engagement should be clearly defined by specifying exactly what the lawyer has agreed to do. It is also helpful to document specifically what the lawyer and client have agreed that the lawyer is not to do for the client.

(2) Fee disputes are a frequent source of disagreement between the lawyer and the client. Professional fees must be reasonable. See Rule 1.5. Most grievances involving fee disputes reveal that the client did not understand how the lawyer's fees were to be calculated and did not understand what expenses would be charged back to the client. To avoid this misunderstanding, the engagement letter should state specifically how professional fees are to be charged, including the hourly or other rates for partners, associates, legal assistants and staff. If a retainer is required, the engagement agreement should state the amount of the retainer, whether any portion of the retainer is refundable and under what circumstances the retainer is refundable.

(3) What expenses are reimbursable by the client is often another source of misunderstanding. If outside lawyers, experts and other professionals are needed, the engagement agreement should state who is required to pay their fees and whether their invoices are to be billed directly to the client or through the lawyer. The engagement agreement should specifically state who, when and under what

circumstances the client is expected to pay court costs, filing fees, witness fees, expert reports, mediation and arbitration fees, appraisal fees, tax and accounting services and whether the client is expected to pay for copying expenses, delivery charges, postage, fax and long distance telephone charges and other administrative, clerical and office expenses.

Charge a Fair Fee. Every lawyer is required to charge a "fair" fee. See <u>Rule 1.5.</u> However, virtually all disputes lawyers have with their clients are really disputes and disagreements over the amount charged. Most lawyers know, but most clients do not understand, that budgeting the total cost of completing most legal engagements is virtually impossible to estimate or project with any degree of accuracy. This fact of life gives rise to many opportunities for misunderstanding and disagreement. To minimize fee disputes and enhance timely collection of invoices, consider adopting the following policies:

(1) Explain your fees and expenses at the beginning of each engagement.

(2) Use a written engagement agreement for every client.

(3) Keep your clients informed about what you are doing and how much time you estimate it will take you to do it.

(4) Send invoices that explain what fees are charged and what was done to generate the fees billed. Include copies of invoices for expenses sought to be reimbursed.

(5) Send invoices at least monthly, if not more often.

(6) Do not let your receivables get too large.

(7) Encourage your clients to ask questions at the time your invoice is rendered, rather than to fester over their questions and concerns. Resolve any fee disagreement quickly.

(8) Encourage prompt communications of conflicts, misunderstandings, disagreements and disputes.

(9) Do not promise specific results.

Be Competent. Every lawyer is required to act with competence. See <u>Rule 1.1.</u> Competence requires that the lawyer learn the facts, know the law and apply the law to those facts, using experience, expertise and common sense. Competence also means giving the client seasoned independent advice. Competence does not mean clairvoyance. Lawyers are not required to know everything or be able to predict accurately every decision or every event that will occur in the course of representing the client. Competence does require the lawyer to:

(1) Get and stay prepared.

(2) Learn the applicable law.

(3) Be inquisitive.

(4) Seek independent confirmation of facts.

(5) Interview the important witnesses in advance of any proceedings.

(6) Analyze critical documents.

(7) Know the client's objectives and the factual and legal basis for the client's position.

(8) Learn the opponent's positions and objectives.

(9) Evaluate the strengths and weaknesses of each party's position.

(10) Explore alternatives for settlement.

(11) Consider creative solutions.

(12) Analyze the risks and benefits of each alternative with the client.

(13) Evaluate the likely results of each alternative for the client.

To avoid grievances alleging incompetence and/or negligence, consider and practice the following:

(1) Do not take on more than you can reasonably handle with professional skill.

(2) Treat every engagement as worthy of your best efforts.

(3) Treat every client with the respect that you would expect if you were the client.

(4) Keep the client informed.

(5) Seek "buy-in" from the client on all tactics and strategies.

(6) Do not promise particular results; promise only your good faith effort.

Follow the Golden Rule. Many lawyers do not take the time or make the necessary effort to treat their clients with common courtesy and respect. Follow the Golden Rule: Do to others what you expect others to do to you. Treat your clients and others with respect and in the same way you would expect to be treated if you were paying the bills. See Rule 1.2.

Communicate Frequently and Effectively. The lawyer's failure to communicate effectively and failure to keep the client timely informed elevates the clients' anxiety and creates uncertainty and disrespect toward the lawyer and the legal profession. See Rule 1.4. Clients can handle bad news. Uncertainty creates pressure and anxiety. It is easy to correct this deficiency. Commit to:

(1) Keep your clients informed promptly after events occur.

(2) Return all phone calls and emails at least daily.

(3) Copy clients with all correspondence, pleadings and other documents.

(4) Tell the client what you expect might happen, but do not promise specific results.

(5) When things change, inform your client.

(6) Promise reasonable deadlines.

(7) Meet your deadlines.

(8) Explain what happened if you miss a deadline.

Be Honest. Lawyers are expected and required to act honestly. Honesty by lawyers is the very foundation upon with the Rule of Law rests. Personal integrity of the lawyers involved in the administration of the law is a bed rock principle. Clients must trust their counsel before they act on counsel's advice. Courts rely upon the truth in pleadings and presentations by the lawyers before them. Opposing parties and opposing counsel are also expected to act with honesty, integrity and candor. "Little lies have many brothers and sisters." "A half-truth is a whole lie." "Spinning the truth is not the truth." Tell the truth and require others to do so too. Honesty is not only the best policy; it is the only policy. See <u>Rules 1.2, 3.1, 3.3, 4.1, 7.1, 8.1, 8.2</u> and <u>8.4.</u>

<u>Avoid Becoming an Involuntary Volunteer.</u> The old saying, "No good deed goes unpunished," is too often true. Many grievances are filed against lawyers who volunteer to help someone out in difficult circumstances without carefully understanding the nature of the relationship or the expectation of the person in need. While being a "Good Samaritan" is praiseworthy, people in need of help often misuse others for their own benefit and expect the unobtainable. All too often these same people in need are the first to complain when their desires or expectations are not met or exceeded. Help others when appropriate, but do so openly and with a clear understanding of the scope of your involvement, the fees to be charged and the expenses to be reimbursed. See <u>Rules 1.1</u> and <u>2.1.</u>

<u>Trust Your Instincts.</u> Accept clients with care. Do not accept an engagement if your instinct tells you to avoid it, for whatever reason. Helping a family member or friend of a friend, accepting a matter against your better judgment, stepping in at the last moment when time does not permit you to render a reasoned legal analysis or careful legal representation, or agreeing to help a person you know will be next to impossible to please are classic examples ripe for later grievances. Just say NO to certain persons, especially if you believe that a conflict of interest could arise or where you have strong personal beliefs which are contrary to those of the client. Do not to accept a client if you do not trust the person. Your instincts are usually correct. Trust your instincts. See <u>Rules 1.1</u> and <u>1.7.</u>

Most lawyers become lawyers to help others in their times of trouble. Most lawyers are compassionate and caring, wanting to see justice prevail. However, the attorney-client relationship is an important relationship. Conflicts and disagreements often arise and become grievances between the client and the lawyer when the nature of the attorney-client relationship is not sufficiently explained, when the scope of services is not clearly defined, when the fees to be charged and the expenses to be reimbursed are not clearly defined or when communications from the lawyer to the client are not prompt and clear and carefully explained. Lawyers must take care to make sure that the client understands at the beginning of and throughout every engagement.

Lawyers are expected to be effective communicators, not just in resolving the client's problems but also in dealing with the client and the client's expectations and obligations. Adopt these suggestions and you will avoid unnecessary disputes and possible grievances. Failure to adopt these simple suggestions will often lead to grievances which could easily have been avoided.

THE GORILLA AND THE BASKETBALL: PERCEPTION vs TRUTH

I recently experienced an AHAH moment. In June, 2007 I attended an awesome seminar entitled "Mediating the Complex Case" at Pepperdine University. After two wonderful days of instruction on the techniques for resolving disputes involving multiple parties through mediation rather than litigation, the Saturday morning class started with a 27 second video. See Surprising Studies of Visual Awareness, www.viscog.com.

There were 28 people in my class, 4 of whom were women. Though I may have been the oldest, I was probably the least qualified to be in this class. The women were a full-time Pepperdine Law School Professor of Mediation; a former US Attorney for Central Los Angeles; a psychiatrist/lawyer/family counselor; and a former insurance executive. The men were mostly trial lawyers, full-time mediators or sitting trial judges in California with more than 25 years on the bench. One of the men was in charge of all government mediations for Hong Kong, and another was in charge of all government mediations in New Zealand. This was a really distinguished group.

Our instructors were Bruce Edwards, who specializes in mediating construction disputes, and Teresa Wakeen, who was mediating many disputes involving sexual misconduct allegations against Catholic priests and bishops. Both had successfully conducted more than 3,000 mediations.

Teresa opened Saturday morning's session with a 27 second video. She said we would see 3 people dressed all in black and 3 people dressed in white T-shirts and black pants. The people wearing white T-shirts were bouncing and passing a white basketball. All 6 people were on a stage. The video camera was stationary focused on the center of the stage. Teresa asked the class to count the number of passes and bounces of the white basketball. At least that is what I heard the instructions to be. She showed the video and then she asked, "How many did you get?" The range of answers was from 19 to 34. Then she showed the video again, with the same instructions. Again the range was from 19 to 34. Finally, Teresa showed the video a third time, but this time with new instructions: Lean back in your seat and see what you see. I was shocked and astounded. A white woman with long black hair and dressed in a black gorilla suit walked from the right side of the stage to the middle, turned and faced the camera, waived and walked off the stage to the left. Not one person saw the gorilla the first two times the video was shown. Teresa explained that people, especially lawyers, are often so focused on one thing, counting the bounces and passes, that they sometimes do not see the obvious: They do not see the gorilla. They are focused on white, and their minds unconsciously blot out what is black.

But I asked, "What is the right answer?" Teresa looked at me and said, "I do not care." The point was that mediators are trained to find the "the gorilla in the room" to assist adverse parties resolve their disputes. But I persisted, "Why was there such a disparity in the answers?" I discovered that some of us heard the instruction to be: "Count the passes and the bounces." Others heard the instruction to be: "Count the changes of possession." Three dribbles and a pass for me was 4, but for others three dribbles and a pass was only one. Not only did I miss the gorilla, but some of us, perhaps even me, completely missed the question. WOW! Perception is sometimes not the truth!

What are the lessons to be learned from the gorilla and the basketball?

1. **MY "TRUTH" MAY NOT BE "THE TRUTH."**

   (a) The facts are illusive. Therefore, the truth is illusive.

   (b) What is true is often different from what we perceive.

   (c) For most people, truth is what they see, hear, feel, touch and smell.

   (d) For most people, "truth" is what they perceive.

   (e) The "truth" may be hidden right in front of your eyes.

2. **SOLVING DISPUTES REQUIRES FINDING THE FACTS.**

   (a) The facts usually control the result.

   (b) If we can agree on the facts, we can usually find an amicable solution.

   (c) Determining what the facts really are is often difficult and illusive.

   (d) Finding the gorilla in the room helps to uncover the true facts and what lies behind the positions of the parties.

   (e) Sometimes the parties do not want you to know the true facts.

3. PERCEPTION CAN CLOUD THE TRUTH.

(a) Lawyers are focused on advancing the positions of their clients.

(b) Focus shapes perception.

(c) Perception influences position.

(d) Position often blurs the truth.

(e) Focus can cloud the truth and keep you from seeing the gorilla.

(f) Your "truth" may simply reflect your focus, not <u>the</u> truth.

(g) What we perceive may be very far from the real "truth." I did not see the gorilla twice.

4. UNDERSTAND YOUR FOCUS TO AVOID MISSING THE GORILLA.

(a) Clients set the focus/objectives for the lawyers.

(b) Lawyers are engaged to accomplish the client's goals.

(c) Perception, background and desired results usually determine position.

(d) What is behind a position often reveals a bias.

(e) Listen carefully to what is said and what is not said.

(f) Most clients do not accept responsibility for their own misconduct.

(f) How things are said reflect attitude and position.

In summary, the parties to a dispute often miss the gorilla, because their position may reflect a specific desired result, not because they are lying (though that is still possible) and not because they are blind to the "truth" (though that is also possible), but rather because the desired result tilts their perception, often without them even knowing it, and perception molds their position.

In seeking to solve problems, uncovering the "true" facts often requires challenging each party's perceptions, positions, postures and principles, but that challenge does not require a personal attack upon the person holding those perceptions. In order to assist our clients in resolving their problems, disputes and conflicts:

(a) Take issue with <u>recollection</u>, not with people.

(b) Take issue with <u>testimony</u>, not with people.

(c) Take issue with <u>posturing</u>, not with people.

(d) Take issue with <u>perception</u>, not with people.

(e) Take issue with <u>positions</u>, not with people.

(f) Take issue with <u>policies</u>, not with people.

(g) Take issue with <u>principles</u>, not with people.

Almost always, when we find the gorilla in the room, the subject which is truly behind the dispute but which neither your client nor the opponent will discuss, we are almost always able to resolve the dispute amicably.

Dr. Tony Evans, a prominent preacher, spoke at the 1995 Promise Keepers event in Dallas. Dr. Evans said that if we want to have a better home, a better family, a better neighbor, a better community, a better city, a better state, a better nation and a better world, it starts with each of us being a better person. The same is true for the legal profession. If we want more respect from the public, each of us has to earn it. If we want a higher level of professionalism practiced by individual lawyers, it starts with each one of us practicing and living the principles of professionalism.

The truth is what truth is, not what you perceive it to be. The truth is that there was a gorilla in the video, even if none of us saw it. The truth is real, factual, objective, provable and measurable. The truth is not what it ought to be or what you hope it is. The truth is not a matter of opinion. There is not a plaintiff's truth and a defendant's truth. There is not a Republican truth and a Democratic truth. Truth is truth, no matter how many deny it and no matter who says otherwise. The truth is not false, just because no one believes it. The world is round, even if the Church and most people denied it. The truth is still the truth, even if no one believes it. The truth is not subject to a majority vote. Lawyers are largely responsible for upholding the truth in the legal system. Truth is the foundation upon which the Rule of Law rests. Find the truth and the truth will make us free indeed.

THE INVISIBLE GORILLA AND OTHER WAYS OUR INTUITIONS DECEIVE US:

A SUMMARY

In the November, 2007 <u>Tulsa Lawyer</u>, I wrote about the "Gorilla and the Basketball," an AHAH moment that occurred to me while attending a CLE program on Mediating the Complex Case at Pepperdine University's Strauss Institute of Dispute Resolution. The psychology professionals who created that now famous illusion, Christopher Chabris and Daniel Simons, have written a new book which contains startling insights about our intuitions and our assumptions. Every lawyer should read *The Invisible Gorilla and Other Ways Our Intuitions Deceive Us ("The Invisible Gorilla")* published by Crown Publishers, New York, June, 2010.

The authors identify 6 commonly held beliefs which often turn out to be simply wrong:

1. **Illusion of Attention.** We believe that what we perceive is what actually happens. However, what we perceive to be is not necessarily what actually is. Our perception is not necessarily the truth. This is especially true when we are intensely focused or concentrating on something else. When we are asked to count the number of bounces and passes of the white basketball between persons dressed in white T-shirts, we often miss the black gorilla in their midst. The unseen car approaching the intersection and the failure of inspectors to identify weapons in suit cases are other examples of the Illusion of Attention. When our attention is focused on one thing, we often miss another thing right before our eyes, especially when what occurs is totally unexpected. This is one reason that eye witness testimony often proves to be very unreliable.

2. **Illusion of Memory.** We believe that our memories are accurate, vivid and substantially complete, but science does not support this intuitive belief. The Illusion of Memory occurs when what we remember is different from what we think we remember. Science has learned that what is stored in our memories is not a replica of reality, but is instead a re-creation of what we perceived. Our memories are shaped and influenced by what we perceived in the first place, but also by what we desire the facts to be, how much time has passed, what our interests are and a host of other factors. Coach Bobby Knight scolded one of his players, and his conduct resulted in Coach Knight being fired as head basketball coach at Indiana. What he remembers of the event and what others who were present remember are significantly different, not because of dishonesty, but rather because of the Illusion of Memory. Mistakes in movies occur when scenes are photographed several times and then spliced together. "Change blindness" is the inability to catch minor differences or mistakes that occur between multiple takes. Most people believe that they will detect unexpected changes, but almost no one actually catches every change, even trained professionals. In fact, vivid details given by eye witnesses to unexpected events often reveal intentional or unintentional distortions, embellishments or reconstructions of those events. Often these reconstructed "memories" reflect subconscious alterations based upon our emotional involvement or our personal stake in those events.

3. **Illusion of Confidence.** Confidence does not necessarily indicate competence, but we think that it does. We treat confidence as a signal of professional skill, accurate memory and expert knowledge; but confidence can be deceptive and is often an illusion. Experience does not guarantee expertise, and confidence does not imply intelligence. Decisions are often made based upon appearances,

personalities, assertiveness and other factors that do not necessarily reflect sound judgment. Jennifer Thompson was a rape victim who testified very confidently when she positively identified her rapist, but she was wrong. Her confidence resulted in an incorrect verdict and 20 years of imprisonment of the wrong man. Confidence does not demonstrate competence, despite our intuition to the contrary.

4. **Illusion of Knowledge.** When people claim to know more than they really do, they suffer from the Illusion of Knowledge. The small boy who constantly asks his father, "Why?" quickly uncovers the lack of the father's knowledge about every day events which the father claims to know intimately. The father's experience and professed knowledge are often much more limited than even he is willing to admit. Experts have often been very wrong. The gross under-estimates by experts in the time and amount of money required to complete a new engineering project illustrate vividly the Illusion of Knowledge. Further, short-term information often distorts long-term results. Stock markets react instantaneously on information tips of the day, but portfolios based upon daily trading usually underperform portfolios based on reliable facts and long-term objectives. We tend to trust experts, even when they opine on questions not within their area of expertise. We have an insatiable desire for instant gratification and sound bites, even though we know from experience that many of those sound bites prove to be very deceptive. The Illusion of Knowledge often persists, even in the face of contrary proven knowledge.

5. **Illusion of Cause.** The Illusion of Cause arises when we see patterns of random events or when we base conclusions solely upon the sequence of other events, even when those events have nothing to do with the conclusions we reach. Our intuition is that the cause of an event can be detected from patterns of other events. We believe

that changes in the weather actually cause pain to increase in arthritis and sinus headaches, even when scientific tests conclusively reveal no causal connection exists. The mother of an autistic child testifies that her child got better after taking a particular medicine, so other parents of autistic children are convinced of the medicine's effectiveness, even when scientific evidence demonstrates conclusively that the medicine had no effect on autism. Personal stories are much more persuasive than statistics or scientific studies, even in the face of conclusive evidence to the contrary. Similarly, experienced trial lawyers know that chronological presentations of "evidence" can be very persuasive, even when the sequence of those events clearly do not prove causation. Causation is proven only by testing the random events and the sequence of events against the conclusion.

6.**Illusion of Potential.** We believe that every human mind contains an untapped resource of unlimited potential just waiting to be tapped, if only we could find the right key; and we want that potential to be available without much effort. It is commonly believed that playing Mozart in the background at work increases productivity or playing Mozart during pregnancy increases the likelihood of the child's later success. The "Mozart Effect" has been widely hailed and disseminated as being the key to increased productivity, performance and higher levels of intelligence, despite repeated scientific studies to the contrary. The Mozart Effect is an example of the Illusion of Potential. We all want a quick fix, a simple pill, an easy road to success; but learning and improvement require focused effort, concentration and practice. Even then most of us could never play the Moonlight Sonata, no matter how much we practiced the piano. While each of us has untapped potential, maximized performance requires concerted effort. There are no quick fixes.

The Invisible Gorilla informs, excites, mystifies and explains much of what we believe intuitively, but our intuitions are often wrong. The more we know about how our intuitions tend to blur and even distort the truth, consciously or unconsciously, the better lawyers we will be and the better people we will become. *The Invisible Gorilla* should be mandatory reading for every lawyer.

STRESS BUSTERS

Lawyers are stressed and many are stressed to their breaking point.* They have too much work to do, they experience too little control over their lives, they receive little or no recognition or reward for their best efforts, and they are constantly in a battle for their clients or with other counsel and with others. They are constantly in negative, emotional, cynical and even angry situations. Many lawyers experience physical, mental and emotional fatigue, if not complete exhaustion. And lawyers are constantly being pulled in many good directions, each deserving the lawyer's best efforts, talent, experience and expertise. Unless lawyers effectively deal with their stress, their best efforts will be diminished and their judgment maybe adversely affected.

Effectively dealing with stress requires identifying the sources of stress and consciously taking practical steps to reduce the stress and its impact. Here I identify some common sources of stress for lawyers, and I offer some practical ways to reduce that stress.**

The following are some but not all of the common sources of stress felt by most practicing lawyers:

The World. Our growing interdependence causes conflicts of increasing frequency and complexity. The world is in turmoil. Terrorism, natural disasters, political corruption and a host of other societal problems fill our days. The pace of the world continues to accelerate. Advancing technologies enable us to work faster and instantly communicate on a real time basis, but clients have come to expect instant solutions to complicated problems. Many clients believe that there are no accidents any more, but few of us accept responsibility for the bad things that do happen to us. If damage or injury occurs or something goes wrong, it must be someone else's fault. Lawyers assist the injured find a remedy for their loss. When instant solutions do not arise or do not satisfy, stress builds for the lawyer.

The Practice. Clients have real problems that do not solve themselves. Solving these problems is inherently stressful. Clients expect and deserve their lawyer's best efforts, experience and expertise. Trials, motion hearings, settlement conferences and filing deadlines inherently impose stress on the lawyer. Excellence in research, writing, negotiation, presentation and performance always takes longer than doing as little as possible to solve the problem. The pursuit of excellence always causes stress. It always takes longer for the lawyer to do his or her best work.

The adversary system results in stress. Clients themselves can be extremely emotional and difficult, and opposing counsel are working to protect and enhance the positions of their clients at the expense of the opposing party. Competition among lawyers has increased dramatically with the increasing numbers of lawyers. Law firms expect associates and partners to devote more and more time at the office and to collect more and more fees for the firm. As a result, many lawyers are pushed to the breaking point.

Perception of the Profession. Once viewed with the highest respect by the public, lawyers are now more often viewed as self-interested and more part of the problem than part of the solution. Lawyer jokes abound, in large part, because they are funny and because there is some truth in them, at least as it relates to some individual lawyers. The media portrays lawyers as sneaky, cynical, overly aggressive and sometimes completely unscrupulous. When cynicism, criticism and ridicule of the legal profession increases, individual lawyers feel more stress.

Family. Our families want, need and deserve our personal presence and our undivided attention. Spouses now work multiple jobs to attempt to satisfy our insatiable and never quenched appetites for more, bigger, faster, newer and better things. Our kids are expected to participate in and excel at every sport, in every artistic activity and in every other type of competitive and learning activity. The pressures of work leave little or no time just for families to be together. Recreation has become work, not relaxation. When family pressures mount, the lawyer often is seen as the cause. When we do not take time to relax, stress mounts.

Professional, Community and Church Activities. Lawyers are expected to participate in bar association activities that advance the profession, in pro bono activities that assist those in need and in community, religious and other charitable and non-for-profit causes that benefit the public and society as a whole. These needs are compelling, time-consuming and often quite stressful; and they take time away from billable hours and from essential family activities.

Self. The pace of life in the practice virtually eliminates opportunities for individual quiet time, for prayer and daily devotions or for spiritual reflection and self-improvement. Everyone needs some alone time for reflection, contemplation and relaxation; but the increasing pressures and demands of daily living can easily suck the marrow out of living a life that matters.

Here are my **Top Twenty Five Stress Busters** in no particular order:

1. **Passionately Pursue God's Presence.** Seek your God and His presence in all you do. Ground every choice, every action and every decision you make on His will. Consciously spend some of each day with your God. By acknowledging the importance of the spiritual

side of your life, some of the financial, family, emotional and professional stress you feel will be placed into prospective. Spirit trumps stress every time.

2. **Pray**. Take time to be with your God every day and during the day. Practice daily devotionals. In the morning stillness, before your family gets up, before the activities and anxieties of the day crowd your God out, pray. Give thanks for all that you have. Pray for patience with the conflicts that you face, poise in the face of adversity, opportunities to help others and healing and wholeness for others. Pray for peace for yourself and for others. Let your God help carry you through the day, and He will! Stress will fade away in the face of your prayers.

3. **Serve Others with Gladness.** Service for the benefit of others gives life meaning, purpose and significance. By volunteering, you can enjoy some of the most meaningful experiences in life, especially when your service is for the benefit of those in need and those less fortunate than you. Service diminishes stress.

4. **Be True to Yourself.** You are NOT what you do, you are NOT what you have and you are NOT what others think. You are a slice of the Divine. You were uniquely created for a special purpose that only you can do. Take time to find out who you really are and what your purpose is, and then do it with passion. Identify your burning desires and pursue them with excitement. Peace, joy and happiness will elude you, as long as you are not doing what you were created to be. By being focused on your purpose, what now causes you stress will soon be transformed from being a burden into being a blessing.

5. **Trust Your Instincts.** Let your conscience guide your thoughts, your words and your actions. Do what you know is right. Honesty, integrity and virtue are more to be cherished than success and more

money. When uncertain about what to do, look deep within your own heart, and you will find the right answer, if you listen and obey. I ask myself: "Would my father approve?" "Will I be proud of myself for doing this?" Doing what is right eliminates the stress of guilt from doing what is not.

6. **Follow Proven Truths and Principles**. Define your core values upon proven principles. Measure your daily choices and actions against those values. Set your goals above easy expectations. Reach beyond your comfort zone. Following time tested values and virtues will maximize your success and minimize any stress in the situation.

7. **Find Balance**. The absence of balance is a major source of stress. There will always be many good demands upon your time, energy and efforts. Your family, profession, community, friends and church all need your special talents and energies. At any given time, one of these priorities will be more pressing than the others. But you must balance those demands to achieve peace in your life. You must prioritize and choose the best, so that you can have the rest. Do not let the demands of others rob you of the peace that comes from finding balance in your life.

8. **Choose Peace.** Stress is the opposite of peace. The pace of life is frantic. The conflicts are many, especially for lawyers who take on the problems of others. In the midst of the turmoil around you, choose peace. Take a deep breath. Pause. Slow down. Simplify. Act with poise. Feel your stress level go down when you choose to be at peace.

9. **Be Positively Joyful.** Celebrate the wonder, awe and mystery of life every moment of every day. Stop to appreciate the world around you. Stress is caused in part by negative, critical and pessimistic conflicts. Consciously nullify the negative by choosing to be optimistic,

positive and full of gratitude for what you have. Minimize the time you spend with people who are critical and negative. Be someone others want to be around. By choosing to be cheerful, stress will flee from you, and joy will fill your life.

10. **Be a Defining Moment for Others.** Your words are important, but you will be known by your actions. Be an example that others want to follow. Character is defined by what you do when no one is watching, and you know that you will not get caught. Do the right thing for the right reason. There is no right way to do what is wrong. Give others encouragement, affirmation and approval, and they will follow you. Being a defining moment for others will give you peace and reduce your stress.

11. **Take Time to Relax.** Nothing relieves stress better than a walk in the park, a fishing trip to your favorite trout stream, skiing the slopes in Colorado, reading an exciting novel on the beach in Florida or just spending time relaxing in your favorite leather chair at home. Calendar a break and do not miss it. Doing something you enjoy will strip stress of its hold on you.

12. **Manage Your Money.** Money or the lack of money causes more stress than just about any other factor in life. Choose to live beneath your expected revenues. You do not need that bigger house, that faster new car, an exotic vacation every six months or the latest technical advancement. Choose to restrain your spending. Save something for tomorrow. By following the simple principle of not spending what you do not have, stress will recede.

13. **Simplify.** The more complicated your schedule, the more stressful your life will be. To the maximum extent possible, simplify your life. Discard what you do not need. Eliminate what you do not use. Reduce your inventory of things to do, meetings to attend,

committees to chair and projects to complete. Just say no when asked to take on a project that you do not have time to do excellently. Focus on what is most important to you, and feel the stress levels decrease.

14. **Do Not Take Everything Personally.** All of us experience disappointments, defeats and disaster. These events are often outside our control. To the extent the result is your fault, take responsibility for it, learn from it and move on. Life happens. Do not take negative events, comments or criticisms too personally. Some people are cynical, angry, sad, disappointed, negative and critical. Do not take their attitude as being a personal attack upon you. Simply avoid them. Stress will subside as you choose not to personalize every bad thing that happens.

15. **Confide in Your Friends.** We are made for relationships with others, not solitude. Find some trusted friends to share your hurts and happiness, to share your joys and disappointments, to share your victories and defeats. By sharing your life with others, you will discover that they have many of the same problems you have and that they have found ways to cope with those stresses and anxieties in ways that can help you cope better. Just sharing in relationship with friends provides you with a reason for hope. Sharing always reduces stress.

16. **Pursue Your Passions**. Spend as much time as possible doing what you enjoy doing the most. If you do not enjoy your job, your committee assignment, your role in church, your responsibilities in other activities, change. You will be less stressed doing what you are good at, what you are called to do, what you enjoy doing the most. Finding your purpose and pursuing your passions will shield you from unhealthy stress.

17. **Laugh**. It is not possible to be stressed out when you are laughing, smiling and having fun. Consciously seek to find fun in all you do and in all you say. Find someone to laugh with. Be someone that others enjoy being with, and your laughter and their joy will suck the stress out of your life and theirs too.

18. **Music/Sing.** Music enables us to share our emotions with others. Music allows us to come alive to the feelings of others and gives us a means to praise and give thanks. Music lifts the very soul of humanity. When down and feeling low, sing a happy song, whistle a joyful tune, hum a few bars of a love song. The music will allow you to come alive and will literally chase the stress away.

19. **Exercise.** Many have found that regular exercise not only strengthens the body but also enlivens the soul. There are many forms of exercise that bring pleasure and peace. Golf, tennis, swimming, rowing, running, yoga and walking are just a few physical activities that reduce stress. When you exercise with another, your frequency and enjoyment increase, and your stress level will fall while your partner's stress level also falls.

20. **Become an Overcomer.** Personal stories of defeats turned into triumphs always reduce stress by reducing your feeling that you are alone in the struggle. There are literally millions of stories of people that have suffered significant adversity only to overcome and triumph through it all. Read stories of those people. Learn from their attitude and experiences. Embrace their optimism and hope into your situation. Stress will disappear as you live out your victories.

21. **Plan to Arrive Early**. Being late is a sign of disrespect to others and brings disrespect and dishonor to you. Being on time reflects that you value others and their time. Few things are more stressful than being late. Do not try to be the last person on the

plane. Do not assume that arriving 20 minutes late is still on time. Simply plan to arrive a little early and feel the tension, anxiety and stress fade.

22. **Prioritize and Organize.** Make a list of what things you have to do and prioritize them. In the process, items that seemed pressing will become less critical, and those that are critical from a timing point of view will be accomplished sooner. In both cases, the level of stress will be reduced as you organize and prioritize.

23. **Schedule Family Time.** Fun with the family can occur in many ways and under many different circumstances. Make a special effort to set aside time to be with each member of your family, both individually and collectively. Take your son to a game and go shopping with your daughter and your spouse. Make a date with your spouse and do not let work interfere. Time specially set aside will demonstrate your love and care for your family, will be cherished by your family and will significantly reduce your stress level at work and at home.

24. **Don't Worry. Be Happy**. Fear, anxiety and worry are choices we make, consciously or unconsciously. A negative attitude, a critical spirit, an angry response create stress. Prepare properly. Think through your action plan. Do what you can control. Then choose to leave worry behind you. Choose to be happy, and watch the stress level diminish in the process.

25. **Learn from the Past.** We have all done things in the past or chosen not to do things with negative consequences. We are disappointed, embarrassed and even guilt ridden. Dwelling on the past will not change the past. Learn from the past and move on. The past is history. The past is past. The future is a mystery. We live in the now. Now is a gift from God. That is why now is called the present. If we

do now what pleases, edifies, builds, enlightens and improves us and others, the past will take care of itself and the future can become perfect.

Life is stressful, and the practice of law adds significantly to that stress. But if we choose to do so, we can reduce our stress and increase our enjoyment of living at the same time. These practical stress-busting suggestions are by no means exclusive. Share your stress-busting suggestions with others and with me at fred@slickerlawfirm.com. Together we can give the legal profession a better name, enhance the professionalism of each lawyer and enhance the public's perception of lawyers as a profession. It is worth the effort.

---

*Lawyers are not alone. The February, 2007 edition of Readers' Digest contains an article entitled, "Burned Out; Has Stress Pushed You Into the Danger Zone?" (Page 153-157). "More than half of workers said they're under a great deal of stress; 77 percent reported feeling burnout sometimes."

**The stress discussed in this article is not to be confused with clinical depression or more serious mental health issues. The Oklahoma Bar Association has established a FREE program of Crisis Intervention Counseling with Life Focus Counseling Services at 405-840-5225 or toll free at 866-762-5252 to assist lawyers 24/7/365 in need of professional advice for lawyers in crisis. Use it when you need help.

AN HONORABLE PROFESSION AND THE GOOD THAT LAWYERS DO

The public's perception of the legal profession is very negative. This perception is, I believe, unfair, inaccurate and untrue. There are many reasons for the negative perception, some of which include the following:

Lawyers charge too much and care too little.

Lawyers profess honesty but act without morality or ethics.

Lawyers are dishonest and spin the truth for their client's benefit.

Lawyers are schemers and tricksters.

Lawyers are sneaky and smart but sharp in a negative way.

Lawyers will take either side, without regard to the truth.

Lawyers are disrespectful, deceptive, rude and arrogant.

Lawyers are rich.

Lawyers prey off of the misfortune of others.

Lawyers are hypocritical.

Lawyers do not explain how fees are charged.

Lawyers do not explain what expenses are reimbursable.

Lawyers do not explain the adjudication process.

Lawyers use legalese without explanation.

Lawyers do not keep clients adequately and timely informed.

Lawyers often ignore and disrespect the client.

The public's perception is formed by the media, which portrays lawyers badly. The public does not understand the adversarial system which pits lawyers against lawyers. The public does not understand the exclusionary rule, which excludes truthful evidence from jury consideration. The public does not know what lawyers really do. The legal process is long, tedious, uncertain and expensive. The client's expectations are often unrealistic. Clients have little contact with lawyers except in crisis. Lawyer jokes demean the profession. The public has no insurance to pay lawyers.

There is some truth in some of these perceptions, but the public's perception of the legal profession as a whole is mostly misguided. Individual lawyers and the legal profession as a whole have not done a persuasive and effective job of informing the public about the good that lawyers do.

The truth is that the legal profession is a learned and honorable profession. Most lawyers are honest, competent, hardworking, caring, compassionate, respectful, effective counselors and public citizens. Most lawyers devote at least some of their time, attention and experience free for charitable, religious or community service projects. Many lawyers are not paid by their own clients for the good work they do, even when the client does not dispute the invoice.

The truth is that lawyers do an enormous amount of good, both for their clients and for the public. Lawyers play a fundamental and an essential role in maintaining public order and in preserving and protecting the Rule of Law. Some but certainly not all of the activities undertaken by lawyers include the following:

Lawyers stand for election to public office, often at great personal sacrifice.

Lawyers write the laws, rules, regulations, codes and standards of conduct to establish and keep the public order.

Lawyers represent the government to insure public safety, order and compliance with law.

Lawyers represent private clients against government over-reaching.

Lawyers represent private clients against criminal charges.

Lawyers represent individuals and organizations in resolving disputes without violence, most often without litigation.

Lawyers give legal advice to the poor, often free and often at great personal inconvenience.

Lawyers mediate peaceful resolution of disputes between adverse parties.

Lawyers volunteer to act as leaders and board members for public agencies, such as school boards, airport authorities, water districts and similar entities, often without compensation.

Lawyers volunteer as leaders and board members for various charitable entities and not-for-profit causes, often without compensation.

Lawyers volunteer as leaders for churches, parishes, synagogues and other religious bodies, serving without compensation.

Lawyers volunteer as teachers, mentors and counselors for educational entities, often without compensation.

Lawyers volunteer as mentors, coaches and leaders to train the youth, usually without compensation.

Lawyers often give free advice in Ask-A-Lawyer and similar informational programs.

Lawyers give enormous amounts of money, time and effort for public, political, civic and charitable purposes.

Lawyers volunteer as speakers at schools and other civic organizations.

Lawyers give money, time and effort to community food banks, day care centers for the homeless, veterans' organizations and similar not-for-profits.

Lawyers provide lawyer referral services to the public at nominal or no cost.

Lawyers have a great story to tell about all the good that individual lawyers do and about what the profession as a whole does to keep our society free and orderly and to advance the principles of equal justice for all. While lawyers are generally excellent at persuasion, the legal profession has not been effective at persuading the public about the good the profession does. We need to do better for the good of the profession and for the good of the Rule of Law.

PROFESSIONALISM OFTEN REQUIRES COURAGE

I recently proposed a definition for professionalism as follows:

"Professionalism for judges and lawyers means possessing, demonstrating and promoting the highest standards of Character, Competence, Compliance, Civility and Citizenship."

This proposed definition was intended to capture concisely all the core values, attributes and characteristics of the professional lawyer. The term "compliance" was intended to mean that the professional lawyer:

1. Complies with all laws, rules and regulations; and

2. Complies with the Rules of Professional Conduct which govern the legal profession; and

3 Complies with generally accepted Standards of Professionalism.

As so defined, however, compliance without qualification would not permit the professional lawyer to challenge by non-compliance unjust, unfair, unequal or unconstitutional laws, rules or regulations. Compliance without some explanation might even prohibit professional lawyers from taking actions necessary to protect their clients. In the extreme, compliance could justify silence or even affirmative support for corrupt, discriminatory and inhuman laws. Of course, that interpretation was not the intended.

When a law unfairly stifles freedom or interferes with equal justice for all or discriminates unfairly against persons because of race, religion, creed or color or violates other fundamental core constitutional principle, non-compliance is not only permitted but may even be mandated. For example, a law that forces people of color to sit on the back row of a public bus should be opposed on equal protection grounds, even in the face of intense public support. Likewise, a law that prohibits marriage between two consenting adults of different races should be challenged, even though there is virtually unanimous community support for the law. A majority does not decide the application of core constitutional principles.

Throughout history, lawyers have led the way in opposing government actions which limit or deny basic human rights. In many instances, these lawyers were forced to challenge accepted but misguided social norms through acts of non-compliance. In virtually all such instances, the lawyers took actions which were both selfless and courageous, a few of which are described below.

Sir Thomas More, Chancellor of England and a Catholic, refused to accept the religious mandate from his friend, King Henry VIII, suffering death rather than compromise his faith. More's example has helped ensure individual religious freedom from government interference for us today. More's moral and ethical struggle was beautifully documented in the movie, <u>A Man for All Seasons.</u>

Our founding fathers, many of whom were lawyers, revolted from oppression by England, declared the 13 colonies independent, established a more perfect union and set the United States on its present quest of individual freedom and equal justice for all. Their revolution was the product of many individual acts of courage and sacrifice in the face of extraordinary risks.

In <u>Marbury v. Madison</u>, Chief Justice John Marshall found a way to declare an act of Congress unconstitutional, thereby establishing the principle of independent judicial review over unconstitutional legislative and executive actions. This opinion faced enormous public criticism and political opposition.

Abraham Lincoln endured almost impossible political and military pressures by outlawing slavery (then the law of the land in many states), by fighting the Civil War and by keeping the United States together as one union under God. His legacy was established through daily acts of courage and self-sacrifice.

In Brown v. Board of Education, Chief Justice Earl Warren lead a unanimous Supreme Court in overturning the long-held doctrine of separate but equal, much to the shock, surprise and criticism of his former political friends. Chief Justice Warren's courage resulted in disruption and disorder in public education but established the greater principle of equality and fairness in public education for all.

Many in Congress courageously forged the legislative compromises required to pass the Civil Rights Act of 1964 at a time of great civil revolt and unrest. Most of those elected officials were lawyers, and many acted courageously against strong opposition from their party and from the public.

Many US attorneys and state district attorneys courageously prosecute allegations of terrorism, public corruption, organized crime, gang violence and other major criminal misconduct at great personal sacrifice, including even treats of violence against them and their families. Their courage, conviction and perseverance are monuments to legal professionalism.

Atticus Finch, the fictional lawyer portrayed in To Kill a Mockingbird, courageously defended a black man wrongly accused of raping a while woman in a small Southern town at great personal risk. He models many public defenders and other lawyers today who, at great personal risk, defend persons wrongly accused of crimes.

Other courageous lawyers devote substantial time and effort to the Innocence Project. They work tirelessly, often against fierce public opinion, to free persons wrongly convicted of serious criminal conduct, thereby helping to protect all of us from wrongful prosecution.

Other examples of lawyers who act courageously include: (1) lawyers who refuse to permit their clients to testify falsely; (2) lawyers who refuse to counsel or permit their clients to commit fraud or a crime; (3) lawyers who refuse to assist their clients in writing and publishing false or misleading disclosure documents; (4) lawyers who represent whistleblowers seeking to prevent serious injury and damages to others; and (5) judges, legislators, public officials and individual lawyers who do the right thing for the right reason, despite enormous contrary public pressures and even personal condemnation from their superiors, friends and family. Evil persists when good men and women remain silent; but individual lawyers help defeat evil by acting with courage in opposing laws which are unfair, unjust or unconstitutional.

Professionalism requires lawyers to comply with all the laws, rules and regulations which govern our society. However, professionalism also requires lawyers to act with courage in opposing laws which are unjust or which produce illicit results.

My proposed definition of professionalism is incomplete without a specific reference to the courage of lawyers who protect, preserve and enhance the Rule of Law. These lawyers serve their clients, sometimes at great personal sacrifice and often exposing themselves and their families to serious risk of harm. Consequently, my proposed definition of professionalism needs to be modified to read as follows:

"Professionalism for judges and lawyers means possessing, demonstrating and promoting the highest standards of Character, Competence, Compliance, <u>Courage</u>, Civility and Citizenship." [Emphasis Added.]

Virtually every lawyer will, at some time during his or her career, be faced with ethical challenges where compliance with the law could produce an unjust result. Our profession encourages all lawyers to act with courage, when the cause is just, despite intense opposition to the contrary. We honor the courage and sacrifice of those lawyers who stand against unfair discrimination and against enforcement of unequal or unconstitutional laws. Their **<u>courage</u>** models professionalism in action.

OKLAHOMA BAR ASSOCIATION'S DEFINITION OF PROFESSIONALISM

Adopted by the Board of Governors on
April 20, 2006

Professionalism for lawyers and judges requires honesty, integrity, competence, civility and public service.

OKLAHOMA BAR ASSOCIATION'S LAWYER'S CREED

Adopted by the Board of Governors on
November 17, 1989; amended March 8, 2008

I revere the Law, the System and the Profession, and I pledge that in my private and professional life, and in my dealings with members of the Bar, I will uphold the dignity and respect of each in my behavior toward others.

In all dealings with members of the Bar, I will be guided by a fundamental sense of integrity and fair play.

I will not abuse the System or the Profession by pursuing or opposing discovery through arbitrariness or for the purpose of harassment or undue delay.

I will not seek accommodation for the rescheduling of any Court setting or discovery unless a legitimate need exists. I will not misrepresent conflicts, nor will I ask for accommodation for the purpose of tactical advantage or undue delay.

In my dealings with the Court and with counsel, as well as others, my word is my bond.

I will readily stipulate to undisputed facts in order to avoid needless costs or inconvenience for any party.

I recognize that my conduct is not governed solely by the Code of Professional Responsibility, but also by standards of fundamental decency and courtesy. Accordingly, I will endeavor to conduct myself in a manner consistent with the Standards of Professionalism as adopted by the Board of Governors.

I will strive to be punctual in communications with others and in honoring scheduled appearances, and I recognize that neglect and tardiness are demeaning to me and to the Profession.

If a member of the Bar makes a just request for cooperation, or seeks scheduling accommodation, I will not arbitrarily or unreasonably withhold consent.

I recognize that a desire to prevail must be tempered with civility. Rude behavior hinders effective advocacy, and, as a member of the Bar, I pledge to adhere to a high standard of conduct which clients, attorneys, the judiciary and the public will admire and respect.

OKLAHOMA BAR ASSOCIATION'S STANDARDS OF PROFESSIONALISM

Approved by the Oklahoma Bar Association
Board of Governors on April 20, 2002
and by the
Oklahoma Judicial Conference on December 20, 2002

PREAMBLE

We judges and lawyers of the State of Oklahoma recognize our responsibility to uphold the longstanding traditions of professionalism and civility within the legal system. The very nature of our adversary system of justice requires respect for the law, the public, the courts, administrative agencies, our clients and each other. While the Rules of Professional Conduct establish the minimum standards a lawyer must meet to avoid discipline, the following Standards of Professionalism represent the level of behavior we expect from each other and the public expects from us in our dealings with the public, the courts, our clients and each other. The Standards of Professionalism are not intended to be used as a basis for discipline by the Court on the Judiciary or the Professional Responsibility Tribunal, or for establishing standards of conduct in an action against a lawyer.

SECTION 1

LAWYERS' RESPONSIBILITIES TO THE PUBLIC

1.1   We understand that the law is a learned profession and that among its tenets are devotion to public service, improvement of the administration of justice, and access to justice for our fellow citizens.

1.2 A lawyer's word should be his or her bond. We will not knowingly misstate, distort or improperly exaggerate any fact, opinion or legal authority, and will not improperly permit our silence or inaction to mislead anyone. Further, if this occurs unintentionally and is later discovered, it will immediately be disclosed or otherwise corrected.

1.3 We will donate legal services to persons unable to afford those services.

1.4 We will participate in organized activities designed to improve the courts, the legal system and the practice of law.

1.5 We will contribute time on a pro bono basis to community activities.

1.6 Our conduct with clients, opposing counsel, parties, witnesses and the public will be honest, professional and civil.

1.7 Our public communications will reflect appropriate civility, professional integrity, personal dignity, and respect for the legal system and the judiciary. However, we may make good faith expressions of dissent or criticism in public or private discussions when the purpose is to promote improvements in the legal system.

1.8 We will not make statements which are false, misleading, or which exaggerate, for example, the amount of damages sought in a lawsuit, actual or potential recoveries in settlement or the lawyer's qualifications, experience or fees.

1.9 We will promptly return telephone calls and respond to correspondence from clients, opposing counsel, unrepresented parties and others.

1.10 We will refrain from engaging in professional conduct which exhibits or is intended to appeal to or engender bias against a person based upon that person's race, color, national origin, ethnicity, religion, gender, sexual orientation or disability.

SECTION 2

LAWYERS' RESPONSIBILITIES TO CLIENTS

2.1 We will be loyal and committed to our client's lawful objectives, but will not permit our loyalty to interfere with giving the client objective and independent advice.

2.2 We will advise our client against pursuing litigation (or any other course of action) that does not have merit.

2.3 We will endeavor to achieve our client's lawful and meritorious objectives expeditiously and as efficiently as possible.

2.4 We will continually engage in legal education and recognize our limitations of knowledge and experience.

2.5 We will reserve the right to determine whether to grant accommodations to opposing counsel in all matters that do not adversely affect a client's lawful objectives.

2.6 We will advise our client, if necessary, that the client has no right to demand that we engage in abusive or offensive conduct and that we will not engage in such conduct.

2.7 We understand, and will impress upon our client, that reasonable people can disagree without being disagreeable; and that effective representation does not require, and in fact is impaired by, conduct which objectively can be characterized as uncivil, rude, abrasive, abusive, vulgar, antagonistic, obstructive or obnoxious. Ill feelings between clients will not dictate or influence a lawyer's attitude, demeanor, behavior or conduct.

2.8 We will always look for opportunities to de-escalate a controversy and bring the parties together.

2.9 We will readily stipulate to undisputed facts in order to avoid needless costs, delay, inconvenience, and strife.

2.10 We will consider whether the client's interests can be adequately served and the controversy more expeditiously and economically resolved by arbitration, mediation or some other form of alternative dispute resolution, or by expedited trial; and we will raise the issue of settlement and alternative dispute resolution as soon as a case can be evaluated and meaningful compromise negotiations can be undertaken.

2.11 When involved in an alternative dispute resolution process, we will participate in good faith, and will not use the process for the purpose of delay or for any other improper purpose.

2.12 We will not falsely hold out the possibility of settlement as a means to adjourn discovery or delay trial.

SECTION 3

LAWYERS' RESPONSIBILITIES TO OTHER LAWYERS

3.1 Communications with Adversaries

a. We will be civil, courteous, respectful, honest and fair in communicating with adversaries, orally and in writing.

b. We will promptly return telephone calls and respond to correspondence reasonably requiring a response.

c. The timing and manner of service of papers will not be designed to annoy, inconvenience or cause disadvantage to the person receiving the papers; and papers will not be served at a time or in a manner designed to take advantage of an adversary's known absence from the office.

d. We will not write letters ascribing to an opposing lawyer a position that lawyer has not taken, creating a "record" of events that have not occurred, or otherwise seeking to create an unjustified inference based on that lawyer's statements or conduct.

e. Unless specifically permitted or invited by the court, copies of correspondence between counsel will not be sent to a judge or administrative agency.

3.2 Discovery

a. General

(1) A reasonable effort should be made to conduct discovery by agreement.

(2) We will not use discovery, the scheduling of discovery, or the discovery process to annoy or harass opposing counsel, to generate needless expense, or as a means of delaying the timely, efficient and cost-effective resolution of a dispute.

(3) We will comply with reasonable discovery requests.

(4) We will object to discovery requests only when we have a good-faith belief in the merit of the objection; and we will not object solely for the purpose of withholding or delaying the disclosure of relevant information or documents.

(5) We will agree to reasonable requests for extensions of deadlines, scheduling changes and other accommodations, provided the client's legitimate rights and interests will not be adversely affected.

(6) We will seek court sanctions or disqualification only after conducting a diligent investigation, and then only when justified by the circumstances and necessary to protect the client's legitimate and lawful interests.

b. Depositions

(1) We will take depositions only when actually needed to ascertain facts or information or to preserve testimony.

(2) In scheduling depositions, reasonable consideration will be given to accommodating schedules of opposing counsel and the deponent (both professional and personal schedules), when it is possible to do so without prejudicing the client's rights. When practical, we will consult with opposing counsel before scheduling any deposition. If a request is made to schedule a time for a deposition, the lawyer to whom the request is made should confirm that the proposed time is available or advise of a conflict within a reasonable time (preferably the same business day, but in any event, before the end of the following business day).

(3) When a deposition is scheduled and noticed by another party for the reasonably near future, a lawyer ordinarily should not schedule another deposition for an earlier date without the agreement of opposing counsel.

(4) We will delay a deposition only for good-faith reasons.

(5) Prompt notice of cancellation of a deposition will be given to opposing counsel.

(6) We will not, even when called upon by a client to do so, abuse others or indulge in offensive conduct directed to other counsel, parties or witnesses. We will refrain from disparaging personal remarks or acrimony toward other counsel, parties and witnesses; and will treat adverse parties and witnesses with civility and fair consideration.

(7) We will not ask questions about a deponent's personal affairs or which needlessly impugns a deponent's integrity when such questions are irrelevant to the subject matter of the action or proceeding, except that questions on these topics may be asked if they are likely to elicit admissible evidence.

(8) We will avoid repetitive and argumentative questions and those asked solely for the purpose of annoyance or harassment.

(9) We will limit deposition objections to those which are well-founded and permitted by (as applicable) the Oklahoma Discovery Code, the Federal Rules of Civil Procedure, any governing local court rules, and any apposite case law. Any such objections will be stated concisely and in a non-argumentative and non-suggestive manner. We will remember that most objections are preserved and need be made only when the form of a question is defective or when privileged information is sought.

(10) Once a question is asked, we will not, through objections or otherwise, coach the deponent or suggest answers.

(11) We will not direct a deponent to refuse to answer a question unless specifically permitted by (as applicable) 12 O.S. 2001, Section 3230.E.1, or Federal Rule 30(d)(1), F.R.Civ.P.

(12) We will refrain from self-serving speeches during depositions.

(13) We will not engage in any conduct during a deposition which would not be allowed in the presence of a judicial officer, including disparaging personal remarks or acrimony toward opposing counsel or the witness, as well as gestures, facial expressions, audible comment, or other manifestations of approval or disapproval during the testimony of the witness. We will not engage in undignified or discourteous conduct which degrades the legal proceeding or the legal profession. Our clients, colleagues and staff will be admonished to conduct themselves in the same dignified and courteous manner.

c. Document Requests

(1) We will limit requests for production of documents to materials reasonably believed to be needed for the prosecution or defense of an action; and requests will not be made to annoy, embarrass or harass a party or witness, or to impose an undue burden or expense in responding.

(2) We will not draft a request for document production so broadly that it encompasses documents clearly not relevant to the subject matter of the case or proceeding.

(3) When responding to unclear document requests, receiving counsel will make a good-faith effort to discuss the request with opposing counsel to clarify the scope of the request.

(4) In responding to document requests, we will not strain to interpret the request in an artificially-restrictive manner in an attempt to avoid disclosure.

(5) When responding to document requests, we will withhold documents on the basis of privilege only when appropriate.

(6) We will not produce documents in a disorganized or unintelligible manner, or in a manner calculated to conceal or obscure the existence of particular documents.

(7) We will not delay producing documents to prevent opposing counsel from inspecting documents prior to scheduled depositions or for any improper purpose.

d. Interrogatories and Requests for Admissions

(1) We will exercise discriminating judgment in using written discovery requests, and will not use them to annoy, embarrass or harass a party or witness, or to impose undue burden or expense on the opposing party or counsel.

(2) We will read and respond to written discovery requests in a reasonable manner designed to assure that answers and admissions are truly responsive.

(3) When responding to unclear written discovery requests, receiving counsel should have a good-faith discussion with opposing counsel to obviate or limit the scope of any objections to the discovery requests.

(4) We will object to written discovery requests only when a good-faith belief exists in the merit of the objection. Objections will not be made solely for the purpose of withholding relevant information. If a written discovery request is objectionable only in part, we will answer the unobjectionable portion.

3.3 Scheduling

a. We understand and will advise our clients that civility and courtesy in scheduling meetings, hearings and discovery are expected and do not indicate weakness.

b. We will make reasonable efforts to schedule meetings, hearings and discovery by agreement, and will consider the scheduling interests of opposing counsel, the parties, witnesses and the court or agency. Misunderstandings should be avoided by memorializing any agreements reached.

c. We will not arbitrarily or unreasonably withhold consent to a request for scheduling accommodations.

d. We will not engage in delaying tactics in scheduling meetings, hearings and discovery.

e. We will verify the availability of key participants and witnesses either before a meeting, hearing or trial date is set or, if that is not feasible, immediately afterward, and we will promptly notify the court, or other tribunal, and opposing counsel of any problems.

f. We will notify opposing counsel and, if appropriate, the court or other tribunal as early as possible when scheduled meetings, hearings or depositions must be cancelled or rescheduled.

3.4 Continuances and Extensions of Time

a. We will agree, consistent with existing law and court orders, to reasonable requests for extensions of time when the legitimate interests of our clients will not be adversely affected.

b. We will agree to reasonable requests for extensions of time or continuances without requiring motions or other formalities, unless required by court rules.

c. We will agree as a matter of courtesy to first requests for reasonable extensions of time unless time is of the essence.

d. After agreeing to a first extension, we will consider any additional request for extension by balancing the need for prompt resolution of matters against the consideration which should be extended to an adversary's professional and personal schedule, the adversary's willingness to grant reciprocal extensions, the time actually needed for the task, and whether it is likely a court would grant the extension if requested to do so.

e. We understand and will advise clients that the strategy of refusing reasonable requests for extension of time simply to appear "tough" is inappropriate.

f. We will not seek extensions or continuances for the purpose of harassment or extending litigation.

g. We will not condition an agreement to an extension on unfair and extraneous terms. This Standard does not preclude a lawyer from imposing reasonable terms, such as preserving rights that an extension might jeopardize or seeking fair reciprocal scheduling concessions.

h. We will agree to reasonable requests for extensions of time when new counsel is substituted for prior counsel.

3.5 Motion Practice

a. Motions will be filed or opposed only in good faith, and only when the issue cannot otherwise be resolved.

b. Before filing a non-dispositive motion, we will engage in a reasonable effort to resolve the issue. In particular, we will exercise discriminating judgment in filing any discovery motion.

c. We will not engage in conduct which forces opposing counsel to file a motion and then not oppose the motion.

3.6 Non-Party Witnesses

a. Dealings with a non-party witness will be civil, courteous and professional, and designed to instill in that witness an overall favorable impression of the legal system.

b. We will issue a subpoena to a non-party witness only to compel such person's actual appearance at a hearing, trial or deposition, and not for inappropriate tactical or strategic purposes, such as merely to annoy, humiliate, intimidate or harass such individual.

c. When we obtain documents pursuant to a deposition subpoena, we will offer to make copies of the documents available to all other counsel at their expense even if the deposition is cancelled or adjourned.

d. We will take special care to protect a witness under the age of 14 from undue harassment or embarrassment. We also will take special care to ensure that questions are stated in a form which is appropriate to the age and development of the youthful witness.

3.7 Privacy

a. All matters will be handled with due respect for protecting the privacy of parties and non-parties.

b. We will not inquire into, attempt to use, or threaten to use facts concerning private matters relating to any person for the purpose of gaining psychological advantage in a case. Inquiry into sensitive matters which are relevant to an issue should be pursued as narrowly as reasonably possible.

c. If there is a legitimate basis for inquiry into such private matters, we will cooperate in arranging for protective measures designed to assure that the information obtained is disclosed only to persons who need it in order to present the relevant evidence to the court or administrative agency.

3.8 Default Judgment

We will seek a default judgment in a matter in which an appearance has been made or where it is known that the defaulting party is represented by a lawyer with respect to the matter, only after giving the opposing party sufficient advance written notice to permit cure of the alleged default.

3.9 Social Relationships with Judicial Officers, Court-appointed Experts, Administrative Agency Hearing Officers and Agency Board Members

a. We will avoid the appearance of impropriety or bias in our relationships with judicial officers, court-appointed experts, administrative agency hearing officers and agency board members.

b. Prior to appearing before a judicial officer, administrative agency hearing officer or agency board member with whom we have a social relationship or friendship beyond a normal professional association, we will notify opposing counsel (or an unrepresented party) of the relationship.

c. We will disclose to opposing counsel (or an unrepresented opposing party) any social relationship or friendship between the lawyer and any court-appointed expert.

3.10 Negotiation of Business Transactions

a. We will adhere strictly to an express promise or agreement with the opposing lawyer, whether oral or in writing, and will adhere in good faith to any agreement implied by the circumstances or local custom.

b. Business transactions should be negotiated, documented and consummated in an atmosphere of cooperation and informed mutual agreement.

c. Meetings, conferences and closings with opposing lawyers and clients will be scheduled at the most practical location.

d. We will make every effort to appear promptly with our clients at a scheduled meeting; and the lawyer who provides facilities for a meeting will be prepared to receive the opposing lawyer and his or her client at the scheduled time.

e. We will clearly identify, for other counsel or parties, all requested changes and revisions that we make in documents.

f. Correspondence will not be written to ascribe to an opposing lawyer a position he or she has not taken or to create a "record" of events which have not occurred.

SECTION 4

LAWYERS' RESPONSIBILITIES TO THE COURTS AND ADMINISTRATIVE AGENCIES

4.1 We will speak and write civilly and respectfully in all communications with the court or administrative agency.

4.2 We will be punctual and prepared for all appearances so that all conferences, hearings and trials may commence on time.

4.3 We will be considerate of the time constraints and pressures on the court, agency and related staff inherent in their efforts to fulfill their responsibilities.

4.4 We will not engage in conduct which brings disorder or disruption to a proceeding. We will advise our clients and witnesses of the proper conduct expected and required and, to the best of our ability, prevent our clients and witnesses from creating disorder or disruption.

4.5 We will never knowingly misrepresent, mischaracterize, misquote, miscite facts or authorities, or otherwise engage in conduct which misleads the court or agency.

4.6 We will avoid argument or posturing through sending copies of correspondence between counsel to the court or agency, unless specifically permitted or invited by the court or agency.

4.7 Before dates for hearings or trials are set, or if that is not feasible, immediately after such dates have been set, we will attempt to verify the availability of necessary participants and witnesses so we can promptly notify the court or tribunal of any problems.

4.8 We will act and speak civilly and respectfully to all other court and tribunal staff with an awareness that they, too, are an integral part of the system.

4.9 **Writings Submitted to the Court or Tribunal**

a. Written materials submitted to a court or tribunal will be factual and concise, accurately state current law, and fairly represent the party's position without unfairly attacking the opposing party or opposing counsel.

b. Facts that are not properly introduced in the case and part of the record in the proceeding will not be used in briefs or argument.

c. Copies of any submissions to the court or tribunal will be provided simultaneously to opposing counsel by substantially the same method of delivery by which they are provided to the court or tribunal.

d. We will avoid disparaging the intelligence, ethics, morals, integrity, or personal behavior of the opposing party, counsel or witness unless any such characteristics or actions are directly and necessarily at issue in the proceeding.

e. We will promptly submit to opposing counsel for review and approval any written order or judgment proposed by us prior to submitting it for entry by any court or tribunal.

f. We will promptly review and approve, or submit proposed changes, modifications or revisions of, any order or judgment proposed by opposing counsel within a brief time period of its receipt.

g. We will not unreasonably delay the entry of any order or judgment of any court or tribunal.

4.10 *Ex Parte* Communications with the Court

a. Except as permitted in Section 4.10(c) below, we will avoid *ex parte* communications involving the substance of a pending matters with an assigned judge (and members of the judge's staff) and an agency hearing officer or board member in an individual proceeding, whether in person (including social, professional or other contexts), by telephone, and in letters or other forms of written communication, unless such communications relate solely to scheduling or other non-substantive administrative matters, or are made upon advice and consent by all parties, or are otherwise expressly authorized by statute or applicable rule.

b. Even when applicable laws or court or agency rules permit an *ex parte* application or communication to the court or agency, before making any such application or communication, we will make diligent efforts to notify the opposing party or a lawyer known or likely to represent the opposing party; and we will make reasonable efforts to accommodate the schedule of such lawyer to permit the opposing party to be represented.

c. When rules permit an *ex parte* application or communication to the court, hearing officer or board member in an emergency situation, we will make any such application or communication (including an application to shorten an otherwise applicable time period) only when there is a bona fide emergency such that our client will be seriously prejudiced if the application or communication were made with regular notice.

d. We will immediately notify opposing counsel of any oral or written communication with the court or agency.

e. Only lawyers will communicate with a judge or appear in court on substantive matters on behalf of a client. Non-lawyers may communicate with court personnel regarding scheduling matters and other non-substantive matters.

SECTION 5

JUDGES' RESPONSIBILITIES TO LITIGANTS AND LAWYERS

5.1   We will be courteous, respectful and civil to lawyers, parties and witnesses. We will maintain control of the proceedings, recognizing that we have both the obligation and the authority to ensure that all proceedings are conducted in a civil manner.

5.2   If we observe a lawyer being uncivil to another lawyer or others, we will tactfully call it to the attention of the offending lawyer on our own initiative.

5.3   We will not employ hostile, demeaning or humiliating words in opinions or in written or oral communications with lawyers, parties or witnesses.

5.4   We will be punctual in convening all hearings, meetings and conferences; if delayed, we will notify counsel, if possible.

5.5   In scheduling all hearings, meetings and conferences, we will be considerate of time schedules and prior commitments of lawyers, parties and witnesses.

5.6   We will make a reasonable effort to decide promptly all matters presented to us for decision.

5.7   We will give the issues in controversy deliberate, impartial and studied analysis and consideration.

5.8   While endeavoring to resolve disputes efficiently, we will be considerate of the time constraints and pressures imposed on lawyers by the exigencies of litigation practice.

5.9 We recognize that a lawyer has a right and a duty to present a cause fully and properly, and that a party has a right to a fair and impartial hearing. Within the practical limits of time, we will allow lawyers to present proper arguments and to make a complete and accurate record.

5.10 We will not impugn the integrity or professionalism of any lawyer on the basis of the clients whom, or the causes which, that lawyer represents.

5.11 We will do our best to ensure that court personnel act civilly and respectfully toward lawyers, parties and witnesses.

5.12 We will avoid procedures that needlessly increase litigation expense.

SECTION 6

JUDGES' RESPONSIBILITIES TO EACH OTHER

6.1 In all opinions and other written and oral communications, we will refrain from disparaging personal remarks, criticisms, or sarcastic or demeaning comments about a judicial colleague.

6.2 We will endeavor to work with other judges in an effort to foster a spirit of cooperation in furtherance of our mutual goal of promoting and nurturing the administration of justice.

FREDERICK K. SLICKER

Frederick K. Slicker is President of Slicker Law Firm, P.C. in Tulsa, Oklahoma. He has practiced law since 1968. He holds a Bachelor of Arts (1965) and Juris Doctor with Highest Distinction (1968) from the University of Kansas and a Master of Laws from Harvard Law School (1973). From 1968 through 1972, Fred was a Captain in the US Army JAGC where he received the Meritorious Service Award.

Fred has been peer selected with an AV rating and as a Preeminent Lawyer in America by Martindale-Hubbell for many years. He has also been peer selected for listing in "Best Lawyers in America" for Mergers and Acquisitions, Franchising and Business Law. He received the OK Bar Association John A. Shipp Award for Ethics in 2013; the Tulsa County Bar Association Neil E. Bogan Award for Professionalism in 2010; and the TCBA Golden Rule Award in 2013 for distinguished service.

Fred was the 2014 Co-Chairman of the Oklahoma Bar Association Professionalism Committee and is the 2014-15 Chairman of the Tulsa County Bar Association Professionalism Committee. Fred has served the Tulsa County Bar Association as a member of the Board of Directors, and as Chairman of the Corporate Section, Chairman of the Professional Responsibility Committee, Chairman of the Professionalism Committee and Chairman of the Alternate Dispute Resolution Committee and in various other capacities.

Fred is a frequent CLE speaker on business law, mergers and acquisitions, franchising, mediation and legal ethics and professionalism topics. He received mediation training from the American Arbitration Association in Dallas, TX and from Strauss Institute of Dispute Resolution at Pepperdine University in Malibu, CA.

Fred is the author of 5 books: <u>A Practical Guide to Church Bond Financing</u>; <u>Angels All Around</u>; <u>Seeking God's Heart: A Devotional Journey through the Psalms</u>; <u>A Treasury of Truth and Wisdom</u>; and <u>This I Believe.</u> Several of Fred's articles on legal professionalism have been published in the <u>Oklahoma Bar Journal</u> and in the <u>Tulsa Lawyer</u>. For more information, see <u>www.slickerlawfirm.com.</u>

CPSIA information can be obtained
at www.ICGtesting.com
Printed in the USA
FSOW02n2129070416
18970FS